BETWEEN
WALDEN
AND THE
WHIRLWIND

THE CHRISTIAN CHARACTER LIBRARY aims to help Christians live out the biblical mandate to become "salt" and "light" in our world through the witness of Christlike character.

In its radical essence, Christian character is not an accumulation of personal virtues, nor is it a lifestyle—it is a life. It is the life of the risen, living Lord Jesus who expresses His nature through us as we surrender our hearts and lives to Him daily.

As we study His life in the Scriptures and commune with Him in prayer, He removes the veil of our sin-darkened nature and transforms us into His own likeness with ever-increasing glory.

The books in The Christian Character Library have been written with the purpose of encouraging you to model the character of our Lord Jesus Christ in a way that bears fruit in the lives of other people—through the power of a life that reflects

"Christ in you, the hope of glory."

LIVING THE CHRIST-CENTERED LIFE

BETWEEN WALDEN

AND THE

WHIRLWIND

JEAN FLEMING

THE CHRISTIAN CHARACTER LIBRARY

NAVPRESS

A MINISTRY OF THE NAVIGATORS
P.O. Box 6000, Colorado Springs, Colorado 80934

The Navigators is an international, Christian organization. Jesus Christ gave His followers the Great
Commission to go and make disciples (Matthew
28:19). The aim of The Navigators is to help fulfill
that commission by multiplying laborers for Christ
in every nation.

NavPress is the publishing ministry of The Navigators. NavPress publications are tools to help Christians grow. Although publications alone cannot make
disciples or change lives, they can help believers
learn biblical discipleship, and apply what they learn
to their lives and ministries.

© 1985 by Jean Fleming
All rights reserved, including translation
Library of Congress Catalog Card Number:
85-61854
ISBN: 0-89109-520-9
15206

Second printing, 1986

Unless otherwise identified, all Scripture quotations
in the publication are from the *Holy Bible: New
International Version* (NIV). Copyright © 1973, 1978,
1984, International Bible Society. Used by permission of Zondervan Bible Publishers. Other versions
used: *Amplified New Testament* (AMP), © 1954, 1958,
The Lockman Foundation; *King James Version*
(KJV).

Printed in the United States of America

Contents

Author

Jean Fleming and her husband, Roger, live in Colorado Springs with their three teenage children. Roger and Jean are on staff with The Navigators and have served in California, Korea, Okinawa, Arizona, and Washington.

Jean speaks to women's groups and is the author of *A Mother's Heart*, also published by NavPress.

To

Roger Fleming

Mary White

Kathy Yanni

Bern Thompson

———

*friends who encourage me
to write*

Introduction

In 1845, Henry David Thoreau built a tiny cabin beside Walden Pond in Concord, Massachusetts. Thoreau lived in utter simplicity during the two years in which he called that cabin home. His book, *Walden*, stands as a classic in American literature as it presents Thoreau's philosophy of simplifying our environment, needs, and ambitions by redefining pleasure and success.

I read Thoreau's book and yearned to find my own isolated Walden, to enjoy solitude and examine my life and purpose. Soon after, I committed my life to Christ, and a different kind of desire to withdraw into quietness surfaced. I longed to draw apart with God to know Him better, to listen to Him, and to enjoy this new relationship.

9

Accompanying my desire to spend time apart with God came a compelling urge to tell others about Christ, to help and serve people. As I sought to minister to others, areas of need in my own life became apparent. To effectively help others, I would need help myself. Life became busier and busier: a Bible study group for my growth and another with some nonChristians, church services and youth group activities, time spent cultivating friendships to share the Lord, a seminar on how to witness, a prayer group meeting after dinner, an appointment to encourage a new Christian to have a quiet time. The whirlwind began to build.

Activities and disciplines may swirl around us with such velocity that our feet barely touch solid ground. And when we finally experience that brief, still moment in the eye of the hurricane, we sit confused and frustrated, wondering what ever happened to the peace and contentment promised to the Christian.

This book is for Christians struggling to live Christlike lives in the midst of a whirlwind of activities, demands, and responsibilities; for those seeking to develop deeper, secret, inner lives while remaining intensely involved in our needy world. In answer to a search for a simpler lifestyle, I have found focusing the Christian life, not simplifying it, to be the key.

Eternal God,
How do You intend the Christ-life to be lived?
Teach us by Your Spirit; train us by Your providence; inspire us with Your presence; enable us by

Your resurrection power; equip us by Your mighty Word.

Interweave our lives with Christ that we might live and move and have our being in Him. May our lives be consumed in His, and find fullest expression in doing Your will. Draw our fragmented lives together in Yourself.

Amen.

1
In Search of Simple

"Surely the Christian life was meant to be simpler than this," a friend complained to her husband.

I agree. In the twenty some years I've been a Christian, I've received instruction on and been challenged to read my Bible daily, pray without ceasing, do in-depth Bible study regularly, memorize Scripture, meditate day and night, fellowship with other believers, always be ready to give an answer to the questioning unbeliever, give to missions and to the poor, work as unto the Lord, use my time judiciously, give thanks in all circumstances, serve the Body using my gifts to edify others, keep a clean house as a testimony, practice gracious hospitality, submit to my husband, love and train my children, disciple other women, manage finances as a good steward, involve myself in school and community activities, develop and maintain nonChristian friendships, stimulate my mind with careful reading, improve my health through diet and exercise, color coordinate my wardrobe, watch my posture, and "simplify" my life by baking my own bread.

My goal: simplify life

My project for 1982 was to simplify my life. My approach was to tame my schedule and to unclutter my environment. To gain more control over my schedule, I laid out a plan after carefully examining the events of my week. To unclutter my surroundings, I had a garage sale and called the Salvation Army to haul away the leftovers. I reorganized various areas of our home. But was this simpler living? I began to question my goal. What did I mean by "simplify life"?

G. K. Chesterton, an English journalist and author, said, "One great complaint, I think, must stand against the modern upholders of the simple life . . . that they would make us simple in the unimportant things, but complex in the important things."[1]

Thoreau gives us further warning: "There are a thousand hacking at the branches of evil to one who is striking at the root."[2]

Was I simplifying life in the unimportant areas? Was I hacking at the external branches and leaving the root issues untouched? Simplifying life sounded like a clear-cut goal when I began, but now I asked myself what I meant by simple. Did I mean grinding my own grains, raising sheep, and knitting my own socks? No. That may be serene living, but not my idea of simple. Was my concern primarily for economic simplicity? When I said simple, did I mean saving string and eating beans? No. Although those lifestyles may have virtues, I had something else in mind.

As I tried to define my goal, I began a journey, both stimulating and exasperating, that continues to raise questions and stimulate a deeper reevaluation of the most basic aspects of the Christian life.

The question, What do I mean by simple? uncovered a disturbing possibility. As I struggled to define simple, I realized that perhaps my desire was to eliminate the hassle, to control life, to make it more manageable. Having a blazing streak of the escapist in me, was I trying to redefine life minus the stresses and pressures?

This possibility came to me with disturbing clarity as we approached Christmas. 'Twas the week before Christmas and I felt half frustrated and half angry inside. The pre-Christmas pace gathered momentum. Baking projects, church and school activities, shopping, parties, Christmas programs, long, slow-moving lines at the post office—all were sources of irritation.

My schedule was busiest when, as a Christian, I wanted it to be the most tranquil. I longed to sit with an open Bible, Christmas carols playing in the background, and prepare my heart to celebrate Christ's birth. But instead of a peaceful and prepared heart, my spirit churned within me.

Then an incident from a Graham Greene novel came to mind with fresh significance. A renowned architect, concerned only with form, light, and structure, designed a church. The people of the church, dissatisfied with the completed building, replaced his windows with stained glass and redid the interior to better suit their tastes.

When a doctor confronted the angry architect with the proposition that prayer might be more important than architectural perfection, the architect retorted, "Men have prayed in prison, men have prayed in slums and concentration camps. It's only the middle classes who demand to pray in suitable surroundings."[3]

That statement startled me. Was I a bourgeois Christian? Must everything be manageable before I could worship? Did I require "suitable surroundings" to meet Jesus? Did my brand of Christianity demand that I be in control of my schedule if I was to greet Christ's birth in the right spirit? Was I perverting the Christian life?

Unworthy goals
I concluded that simple living wasn't a worthy goal. And neither were some other goals.

To do more. "My problem is that I'm driven," confessed a friend.

We live in a fast-paced, high-pressure society. We demand more and more of ourselves. Whether we compete to shave seconds off seconds in a race, push ourselves to check more off our "do list" than yesterday, or strive to increase our company's production, we live with a stress produced by more, faster, bigger, and better.

But is more necessarily better?

Is faster necessarily better?

Is bigger necessarily better?

Is better necessarily better?

"After all," as Thoreau reminds us, "the man whose horse trots a mile in a minute does not carry the most important message; he is not an evangelist, nor does he come around eating locusts and wild honey. I doubt if Flying Childers ever carried a peck of corn to mill."[4]

The question is not, How can I do more? but, Am I doing the right thing?

To master life. A Christian acquaintance once asked me if I felt I had life "all together." The answer I gave surprised, perhaps even shocked, her. "I don't *ever* expect to feel like I have it all together."

I think the intent of her question was *mastery.* Have you mastered the relationships and responsibilities within your home, church, and beyond? Have you arrived at that longed-for, comfortable point where struggling, striving, and failure are exiles?

I have not arrived.

Jesus has not asked me to have it *all together.* Here on earth no one arrives. All Christians are en route. The most mature press toward the mark; some of us stumble and shuffle along. Only when we see Jesus in Heaven will we be truly like Him (1 John 3:2).

To keep life in balance. Knowing my husband was committed to our children, I expressed my concern that we were away from home more evenings a week than I felt best for the family.

"I understand how you feel," Roger told me. "I agree that this shouldn't be our pattern, but I believe God has directed in these involvements. It means that for a few months life will be out of balance."

Mothers of young children seldom get enough rest. Illness, a new job, or a move may pull life out of balance.

To control life. My passion for horses and my callowness commingled for an exciting equestrian experience. Pure, joyous ignorance mounted Lucky Charm (a misnomer) that spring day. Not many minutes into that ride, Lucky Charm broke into a gallop, zigzagged through trees, ignored the screams and curses of golfers as she raced up the fairway, across a field, through the woods, and broke out onto a cement road. Lucky Charm's hooves sparked and thundered beneath me. Trees, bushes, even life itself, raced by me. I was on board, but Lucky Charm was in control.

Sometimes life seems like a runaway ride. Circumstances race on beyond our control. We bounce around, frantically clutching for the reins, never quite getting a firm hold on them. But God has not asked me to maintain complete control.

To organize life. Every year hordes of new books, replete with everything you ever wanted to know about organizing life, crowd onto the shelves. Buyers feverishly purchase these wonder drugs, which promise to stamp out the dread disease of disorganization. I've read my share, but even so, I'm still disorganized much of the time.

In my search for simple, I had hacked at some of the "branches." Now I was ready to "strike at the root."

Notes

1. Gilbert K. Chesterton, *Heretics* (New York: John Lane Company, 1905), page 136.
2. Henry David Thoreau, *Walden and Other Writings*, ed. Joseph Wood Krutch (New York: Bantam Books, 1962), page 161.
3. Graham Greene, *A Burnt-Out Case* (New York: The Viking Press, 1961), page 51.
4. Thoreau, page 144.

2
Focusing Life

Whatever had stirred my pursuit of simplicity in the beginning continued to press me on. The stirrings were legitimate, but I knew now that my goal of simplicity, at least in the usual sense, wasn't taking me where I needed to go. The root went deeper. The search convinced me that what I needed was to look beyond an external and superficial answer. The devout Quaker teacher Thomas Kelly said,

> I would suggest that the true explanation of the complexity of our program is an inner one, not an outer one. The outer distractions of our interests reflect an inner lack of integration in our own lives. We are trying to be several selves

at once, without all our selves being organized
by a single, mastering Life within us.[1]

Our attempts to control and regulate life, no
matter how good we are at it, leave the inner man
fragmented still. The simplicity man seeks is not
one of organization and management, but of relationship. Bernard of Clairvaux, a French monk
and hymn writer (1090-1150), said,

> So long, then, as I am not united to God, I am
> divided within myself and at perpetual strife
> within myself. Now this union with God can
> only be secured by love. And the subjection to
> him can only be grounded in humility. And the
> humility can only be the result of knowing and
> believing the truth, that is to say, having the
> right notions of God and of myself.[2]

Thomas Kelly spoke of integrating all of life
under one single, mastering Life. Bernard of
Clairvaux defined the issue as union with God
which grows out of having right notions of God
and of ourselves. E. Stanley Jones expressed it this
way: "A sense of wholeness. Fragmentation was
over. Life was pulled into central meanings and
purposes around a single Center."[3]

The answer for satisfying living for the Christian lies not in organizing, managing, or control-
ling life, but in focusing life. The Bible teaches
that our relationship to God must take absolute
precedence over everything else in life: "But seek
first his kingdom and his righteousness, and all

these things will be given to you as well" (Matthew 6:33).

But what does it mean to "seek first"? Certainly it does not mean sequence. It does not mean seek God first, then scratch that off the list and pursue the rest of life. We never complete our obligation to seek Him. Seeking God first is not a matter of *order,* but of *focus.*

Christ must not become simply another item in our life—not even the most important item. He did not come in order to be the most crucial piece of our fragmented life; He came to absorb all of life—our family, job, talents, dreams, ministry—into Himself and impress on it His mark.

To add Christ to our already-busy life is to complicate living; to allow Christ to absorb all the elements of our life is to simplify it. Life is simplified when there is *one* center, *one* reason, *one* motivation, *one* direction and purpose.

The Apostle Paul's obvious center was Christ. His writings never digress from Christ. They ring with the steady, predictable hammer striking the anvil of life: life is *in* Christ, *of* Christ, *through* Christ, *by* Christ, *with* Christ, *for* Christ, *from* Christ. To live is Christ, and to die is more of Christ.

Paul's life wasn't easy, but it had an unshakable, exultant quality that gave it a clear, fine resonance and a quiet, even stark, simplicity. As Paul applied his hammer-song to all the events and trials of life, he asked only a few fundamental questions: How can I know and experience more of Christ in this situation? What does Christ want me to do? How can this situation bring Him glory and honor?

Making God Director and Audience

To the dancers of the New York City Ballet Company, the late George Balanchine was both director and audience. They so loved, esteemed, and feared him, that no matter how large the crowds, they danced for only one audience: Mr. B. The enthusiastic applause from beyond the lights meant little if Mr. B. was not pleased.

To focus our life in Christ, we must allow Him to become our Director and Audience. The movements of our life must be choreographed by Him, performed for Him.

In the dance of His life on earth, Jesus made the Father His Director. From the first recorded incident of Jesus exerting His will—when as a twelve-year-old boy He remained in Jerusalem at the Temple—to the end of His time on earth, one dominant theme is obvious: "For I have come down from heaven not to do my will but to do the will of him who sent me" (John 6:38).

His purpose was fixed by the Father's will. The young boy, Jesus, said to His mother, Mary, "Why were you searching for me? . . . Didn't you know I had to be in my Father's house [involved in my Father's affairs]?" (Luke 2:49).

We see our Lord faithfully obedient to the Father's direction as Jesus was baptized by John. To overcome John's reluctance, Jesus said, "It is proper for us to do this to fulfill all righteousness"

(Matthew 3:15). After His baptism, Jesus was impelled into the desert to be tempted. He was led away from times of teaching and feeding multitudes to single out a short tax collector in a tree, or a woman with longtime medical problems. He moved at the Father's bidding from the press of the crowds to quiet retreat in an olive grove, from Galilee to Jerusalem to Samaria—and finally to Jerusalem and the cross.

The reason for His coming, the purpose of the journey, was that He might do the Father's will. If He had been unwilling to come under those conditions, there would have been no reason to come. The eternal future of mankind hung on Christ's obedience to the Father. When He faced the agony of the Cross, He struggled, but concluded, "Now my heart is troubled, and what shall I say? 'Father, save me from this hour'? No, it was for this very reason I came to this hour. Father, glorify your name!" (John 12:27-28).

After His resurrection, as He walked the road to Emmaus with two fellow travelers, He said, "Did not the Christ have to suffer these things and then enter his glory?" (Luke 24:26).

To human reasoning, the direction of Jesus' life may not seem advisable or strategic. After Jesus had fed the multitudes, He withdrew by Himself into the hills because He knew the people intended to make Him king (see John 6:14-15). Would that have been so terrible? After all, as king, Jesus would have had high visibility, an influential platform from which to proclaim His message, and the opportunity to reach the highest eschelons of society. But, although He was King, it was not the time or place for His coronation. The Father, Jesus' Director, was ordering His steps.

The Eternal Creator became human and lived thirty-three years on earth in perfect conformance to the Divine Will—not with cringing servility or flaccid resignation, but with a sublime and joyous energy. Jesus' life, the perfect example of life totally and singularly directed by the Father, was full of pleasant fruit. No life before or since has exhibited such inner purity and freedom from conflicting motives and compromised integrity. No thought for His own reputation or gain colored His speech or actions. He was never anything but God's Man on the scene. Jesus said, "He who speaks on his own does so to gain honor for himself, but he who works for the honor of the one who sent him is a man of truth; there is nothing false about him" (John 7:18).

How different from Jesus' life is natural man's. Self interest confuses the issues; clashing motivations distort perceptions. The truth becomes a blur, and it is difficult to distinguish baser goals from best intentions. Man needs one Director.

Just as the Father directed Jesus' life, so He wants to direct our life. Numerous rich promises abound in Scripture proclaiming God's desire and ability to lead us: "I will instruct you and teach you in the way you should go; I will counsel you and watch over you" (Psalm 32:8). "I am the Lord your God, who teaches you what is best for you, who directs you in the way you should go" (Isaiah 48:17).

The decision to make God our Director is critical to our growth and experience of intimacy with Him. Jesus promised, "If any one chooses to do God's will, he will find out whether my teaching comes from God or whether I speak on my own" (John 7:17). Obedicnce to God's will produces a settled assurance of spiritual reality; as we continue in obedience, He promises to reveal Himself to us (John 14:21).

Jesus' revelation of Himself leads us into deeper fellowship with Him. "The one who sent me is with me" Jesus said. "He has not left me alone, for I always do what pleases him" (John 8:29). Christ's obedience secured intimacy with the Father. Our obedience gains an ever deepening relationship as well. Our Director calls us "friends" and makes known His Master's business to us: "You are my friends if you do what I command" (John 15:14).

Jesus startled His listeners when, after they had announced that His mother and brothers were outside looking for Him, He said, "Here are my mother and my brothers. Whoever does God's will is my brother and sister and mother" (Mark 3:35). Obedience is a bond closer than blood.

Jesus' obedience proved His love for the Father: "The world must learn that I love the Father and that I do exactly what my Father has commanded me" (John 14:31). He tells us, "If you love me, you will obey what I command" (John 14:15). A God-directed life is the only sure evidence that we love Him.

Demonstrating our love for God through our

obedience to His direction is the surest indicator of His work in our life, as it was for Jesus: "For the very work that the Father has given me to finish, and which I am doing, testifies that the Father has sent me" (John 5:36). The obvious tenor of Jesus' life was to please the Father. His obedience, both the joy and struggle of doing the Father's bidding, was convincing proof that His work was from and of God. Neither the approval nor the disapproval of people is any sure indicator of the validity of our work; our faithfulness and obedience to God stand as the true test.

Following God's direction

For Jesus, it was one of those whirlwind days—teaching in the synagogue, then healing Peter's mother-in-law, followed by a late-night session with the whole town gathered outside the door. He healed, cast out demons, and squeezed in a short night's sleep.

The next morning, Jesus' companions found Him in a solitary place praying. They excitedly exclaimed, "Everyone is looking for you!" The crowds were back. It was an evangelist's dream come true—a ready and eager audience. What a golden opportunity. But the disciples were astonished by Jesus' response: "Let us go somewhere else—to the nearby villages—so I can preach there also. That is why I have come" (Mark 1:38).

On what basis did Jesus make such a decision?

He had just spent time alone with His Father and received fresh direction. The Scriptures report, "Very early in the morning, while it was still dark,

Jesus got up, left the house and went off to a solitary place, where he prayed" (Mark 1:35). In the quietness of that early morning, in the aftermath of a busy day, Jesus listened for His Father's voice. He did not determine His direction based on human wisdom, current needs and opportunities, man's strategy, or His own personal preference. Jesus had one Director.

The practice of spending time alone with God has been called the Morning Watch, Personal Devotions, and the Quiet Time. By any name, it is essential to the focused life. Make God your Director by setting aside time each day to read the Bible and pray.

God directs us through His Word and His Holy Spirit. They are our Director's gracious provision for us. The Bible is God's most complete revelation of Himself to us. Through it we grow in our understanding of what He is like, what He has done, what His plans are for the future, and what He wants from us. If Christ is to be our Center, our Director, we must develop right notions of God and of ourselves, through His words to us.

God's Holy Spirit lives in every believer. He is our Counselor, Tutor, and Guide—our Director-in-Residence. But His voice is quiet, and our spiritual ears must be trained to listen for His instruction and leading. Before opening your Bible each morning, ask Him to teach you and make clear God's ways and will. Then read with the intent to do whatever He asks of you. Stop and pray over ideas, questions, and commands you encounter in the Bible—and then continue on. Read a chapter each day, reflect on the instructions and encouragements in the passage, and spend some time considering how God wants you to respond.

Roger's mentally retarded brother, Don, has lived with us at various times throughout the years. Each time has brought certain strains and struggles. This last time as I was facing Don's coming yet again, I was already a little weary from other pressures. I asked, "Lord, what do You want from me in this situation?" As I asked that question and listened, the Holy Spirit brought to mind a passage of Scripture (Matthew 25:31-46), and I sensed the Spirit saying, "Treat Don as if he were me."

In these last months, I have had many opportunities to respond to God as my Director or to refuse His leadership. I can take Don a glass of iced tea, encourage him with comments of appreciation, offer to drive him to the bike store to get a part for his bike, buy a special treat when I shop for groceries and leave it on his bed, overlook eccentricities that can irritate—and all the while, remind myself that someday Jesus will say, "Thank you for the iced tea, the trip to the bike store, the bag of peanuts."

But I can also drape the thin arm of self-pity over my drooping shoulders, and convince myself that God is too demanding a Director. I've worked at the former pattern and fallen, at times, into the latter. But in obedience as well as in rebellion, I've become convinced that making God my Director brings simplicity and health.

Living for the right audience

Even after we get God's direction for our life, however, we sometimes end up living out God's will to the wrong audience.

A young missionary wife shared that she hated to come home on furlough. Why? Because after people asked her husband about his work on the foreign field, they would turn to her and ask, "And what do *you* do?" Although she and her husband agreed that while their children were small her contribution should be made in the home, she felt defensive and somehow a failure each time they asked. She was sure they expected more than, "I'm a wife and mother."

This dedicated young woman had left the security of her own country because God had directed. Out of her love for Him, she had obeyed. She and her husband had sought God's will and believed she should invest her time in the home rather than accept a position in the mission office or heavy responsibilities outside the home. But when confronted with the question, And what do you do? it became apparent that God was her Director, but not her Audience.

To understand what it means to make God our Audience, we have only to reflect on the life of Jesus. He stated simply, "I always do what pleases him" (John 8:29). A single center produces a stability unknown to those who vacillate, continually trying to figure out what others expect of them. In Jesus is no hint of swither or wobble, no compromise of integrity to accommodate public opinion. Jesus was absolutely free of self-consciousness and anxious thoughts of how others perceived Him. He focused on pleasing one Audience.

When Jesus said, "I do not accept praise from men" (John 5:41), He did not mean that He will not accept our worship—our praise is appropriate and He delights in it—but that man's approval or disapproval doesn't influence His actions. The Apostle Paul said it this way: "Am I now trying to win the approval of men, or of God? . . . If I were still trying to please men, I would not be a servant of Christ" (Galatians 1:10).

The heart of the issue is *focus*. Jesus Himself asked, "How can you believe if you accept praise from one another, yet make no effort to obtain the praise that comes from the only God?" (John 5:44).

Jesus also warned us, "Be careful not to do your 'acts of righteousness' before men, to be seen by them" (John 6:1). This, of course, does not mean that if you want to take a plate of cookies to the neighbors, you must clandestinely sneak the goodies onto their porch. The issue is focus and motivation. Whose approval are you seeking? Will you be crushed if they never thank you, or are you focusing on another Audience?

There are serious consequences of choosing to live to the wrong audience. In Proverbs 29:25 we read, *"Fear of man will prove to be a snare."* Many of the leaders of Jesus' day believed in Him, "but because of the Pharisees they would not confess their faith for fear that they would be put out of the synagogue; for they loved praise from men more than praise from God" (John 12:42).

Melinda experienced anxiety for days before Jim's boss and wife came to dinner. Bruce rehashed the sales meeting in his mind again and again: How did I come across? Did my responses make me sound uninformed? Did my voice tremble on that hard question? Mike made it through basic training without anyone suspecting he was a Christian. Fear kept Allison from raising her hand when an atheistic professor blustered, "Raise your hand if you are a Christian."

Vital energy is drained away when we are focusing on making a good impression. An attempt to impress produces a duplicity that undermines personal integrity and leaves us feeling hollow inside. To live for the approval of men is to live with tension and anxiety.

Man is a hard audience to please. It is impossible to please all the people all the time; we can't even please one person all the time. Even loving parents can find it difficult to respond rightly when a child surprises them with breakfast in bed and then spills the maple syrup on the bedspread. Or when a child, after hearing Dad talking about how badly the house needs painting, decides to tackle the job himself to lighten the load—but instead of paint, he uses varnish.

The heart was right, but the outcome was a sticky mess. Man looks at the results; God looks at the desire and motive. Since we have such a gracious audience in our God, aren't we foolish to make men our focus?

Francois Fenelon, the Archbishop of Cambrai until 1715, gave good advice when he said,

> Do not be vexed at what people say. Endeavor
> to do the will of God and let them speak. You
> will never succeed in pleasing men, and it would
> not be worth the trouble if you could. . . . We
> must love our fellow beings without depending
> upon their friendship. . . . Fix your attention
> upon God alone in your connection with them.[4]

Even the good we do (pray, fast, give to the poor) receives no reward from the heavenly Father if the motivation is to impress people. When we determine our audience, we determine our reward. If we play our life to men, we receive the kinds of rewards men give; if we focus on pleasing our Father in Heaven, we receive the kinds of rewards God gives.

When God calls us to pray, fast, and give "in secret," He speaks not of the secrecy of the spy, but the secrecy of the lover. He calls us to withdraw from the tensions of pleasing others to His private, hidden, inner garden with luxuriant foliage, bubbling springs, and fragrant blossoms; to leave behind ambition, fear, and reputation and develop an intimate relationship with Him.

A secret shared fosters intimacy. To be the first to know a friend is engaged, is expecting a child, or has received a promotion, makes us feel especially close. In the same way, when we live with the inner purpose of pleasing God in what we say and do, the relationship deepens.

An opportunity to live to God, not man, came one day as I folded a batch of clothes. We were about to leave for one of the children's soccer game, and I was struggling. Don was living with us at the time. He was overweight and usually poorly groomed. Although it was no particular problem to me to have Don accompany us to games when Roger was home, I flinched at inviting him to go this time, since Roger was traveling. The reason? I was afraid someone might think Don was my husband.

I entertained the thought of calling back over my shoulder as we stepped out the door, "Don, we'll be back in a couple of hours." But I knew Don liked to go. And the Lord asked, "Who is your audience?"

I stopped short. What did it matter if strangers thought Don was my husband? Was I seeking man's approval or God's? That afternoon as I walked across the soccer field with Don and the children, I felt a sweet closeness to God. He was my Audience.

Implanted in all men is a sense of what life should be. The purest parts of these dreams will be fulfilled in Heaven. But until then, let us focus on our Director, who shows us the path of life. Let us also live in the presence of our Audience, who bestows fullness of life.

> You have made known to me the path of life; you will fill me with joy in your presence, with eternal pleasures at your right hand (Psalm 16:11).

Notes

1. Thomas R. Kelly, *A Testament of Devotion,*

ed. Douglas V. Steere (Nashville, Tennessee: The Upper Room, 1955), page 13.

2. Bernard of Clairvaux, *The Love of God*, ed. James M. Houston (Portland, Oregon: Multnomah Press, 1983), page 8.

3. E. Stanley Jones, *A Song of Ascents* (Nashville, Tennessee: Abingdon Press, 1968), page 29.

4. Francois Fenelon, *Selections from the Writings of Francois Fenelon*, ed. Thomas S. Kepler (Nashville, Tennessee: The Upper Room, 1962), page 17.

3
Living
Decisively

Alas! As we seek to focus life, a formidable problem becomes apparent. Life loses focus without any effort, determination, or decision on our part. The process of living, day in and day out, tends to dilute and divert focus. We become so busy that we have no time to consider *how* we live. Plato said the unexamined life is a life not worth living. Yet many lives are like flotsam adrift.

However, nothing in Jesus' life resembled aimless drifting. He didn't wander through life; He strode resolutely. He sought His Father's direction and approval. Jesus had a single eye and, consequently, lived decisively. John recorded an example: "Jesus knew that the time had come for him to leave this world and go to the Father. . . .

Jesus knew that the Father had put all things under his power, and that he had come from God and was returning to God; so he . . . began to wash his disciples' feet" (John 13:1-5).

Jesus was ever conscious that His roots were in Heaven, that He had a specific mission on earth, and that He would return to Heaven. With great consciousness of who He was, where He had come from, and where He was going, Jesus washed His disciples' feet and then went to the Cross.

Like ours, Jesus' sojourn on earth had a time restriction and a mission—just so much time to accomplish the assigned task.

Earlier, Jesus' brothers had tried to persuade Him to go to the Feast of Tabernacles, the center of religious activity, and reveal Himself totally. What a temptation to prove who He was to those in His family. It seemed to be good advice, but Jesus' timetable was set by God, not men. He remained steadfastly in step with the Father's plans for His time on earth. He did not charge ahead—or hang back. Jesus said, "The right time for me has not yet come; for you any time is right. The world cannot hate you, but it hates me because I testify that what it does is evil. You go to the Feast. . . . for me the right time has not yet come" (John 7:6-8).

The word *time* means a set season. Jesus knew the Father had a set timetable for His life—a prearranged program that climaxed at the cross. Jesus would not circumvent the Father's plan, though to do so would have, perhaps, been more immediately satisfying.

Sometime after His brothers left, Jesus secretly made His way to the Feast and waited in obscurity until the fourth day. He knew great hostility existed toward Him, yet He preached openly in the Temple. As expected, the Jews tried to seize Him. But the Scriptures record that "no one laid a hand on him, because his time had not yet come" (John 7:30).

Jesus could not be pushed ahead of schedule, and no violence could rush the Father's timing. Jesus lived decisively with a sense of God's timing for His life: "I am with you for only a short time, and then I go to the one who sent me" (John 7:32).

Timing and destiny

God has assigned each of us a time and a task: "All the days ordained for me were written in your book before one of them came to be" (Psalm 139:16). At a time of crisis for the Jews, Mordecai said to Queen Esther, "Who knows but that you have come to royal position for such a time as this?" (Esther 4:14). The Lord told Jeremiah, "Before I formed you in the womb I knew you, before you were born I set you apart; I appointed you as a prophet to the nations" (Jeremiah 1:5). Paul wrote in a letter to the Colossians, "Tell Archippus: 'See to it that you complete the work you have received in the Lord'" (Colossians 4:17).

Recognizing who we are in Christ and aligning our life with God's purpose for us gives a sense of destiny. It enables us to say with Nehemiah, "I am doing a great work." It gives form and direction to our life.

Pruning

Unfortunately, our life may look more like a form-less tangle of limbs and branches than a precisely pruned tree. We struggle to determine which limbs and branches are essential and which are super-fluous; which bear fruit and which merely use nour-ishment. With a carefully pruned tree, the relation-ship of limb to trunk is clear. Periodically, limbs and branches that do not contribute to the life of the tree are cut away. That pruning process can be so painful to the owner of the orchard that he will sometimes have someone else prune his trees.

I view my life as a tree. The trunk represents my relationship to Christ; the limbs represent major areas of God-given responsibility such as family, job, ministry, and personal development; and the branches represent the activities and opportunities of life. Even without special care, activity branches multiply. Soon the profusion of branches becomes more prominent than the trunk and limbs. When this happens, I feel trapped, frustrated, and empty. Why? Because my life is shaped and drained by activities that have lost their pertinence to Christ.

For example, the activities expected of a mother multiply conspiratorially: supervising a school field trip, organizing a car pool for soccer games, baking for the fourth grade bake sale, help-ing a child with fractions, fighting nine yards of yellow net for a costume needed on Friday.

To "sacrifice" for my family is a sincere veneer that wears thin in time. I must go beyond defining life by activities. I must focus not on the branches, but on the trunk and limbs. I *do* what I do because of Jesus and His claim on my life. I *don't do* what I don't do for the same reason.

On a finely pruned tree, the trunk and limbs are prominent. The limbs grow out of my relationship with Christ and sprout many new branches each year. I must examine my tree and determine which branches need to be pruned back or hacked off at the base. Life is always changing. My tree must undergo changes too.

This is the process I use to prune my life. Three or four times a year, I spend half a day with the Lord to evaluate my life, to examine my schedule, and to set some new directions for the months ahead. I spend most of the time reading the Bible, praying, and singing to the Lord. This quiet time acts like a knife to cut through the illusions and mirages of everyday life. It enables me to focus my attention, to set my heart on things above, where Christ is seated at the right hand of God. I set my mind on things above, not on earthly things (see Colossians 3:1-2).

Then I lay out my tree before the Lord. I make lists of current obligations, activities, and opportunities. I pray, "At this point in my life, Lord, what is it you want me to do? What must I do to keep my relationship to You vital? What do You want me to say yes and no to?

Whenever I say yes to something, it means I will be saying no to something else. For example, if I say yes to being treasurer of the P.T.A., it may end up crowding out my time with God, my time with the family, my preparation for Sunday school, or my Sunday afternoon nap.

Looking at life this way helps me insure that I don't become too busy or fragmented to maintain my relationship to the Lord, to have vital time with my family, or to have a part in influencing the world for Christ.

As I evaluate my life before the Lord every three or four months, I remind myself that life is seasonal. There is a time and a season for everything (see Ecclesiastes 3:1). I can't do everything at once, nor should I. The question is, At this point in my life—what *should* I be doing?

A man with a demanding new job may decide not to play on the church softball team or to tackle a remodeling project during that initial four to six-month period, even though he loves softball and considers the remodeling project a high priority. A mother of young children, who dreams of finishing her college degree, may put off returning to school without frustration if she evaluates her life for the right timing.

The result of this half day of seeking God's direction isn't always a clear sense of what I should do. But as I spend this time listening for His voice, sitting on the edge of my chair straining forward spiritually to hear what He wants to say to me, I bring my heart into alignment with God. Even when I'm unsure of the next steps to take, the time apart confirms my desire to allow Him to lead, and my commitment to follow. Spending that time helps me to think God's way. He says my relationship to Himself and to others is important. So is my growing more like Jesus in character.

Jesus did not heal everyone. He did not meet the needs of all the poor, or cast out all demons. I cannot meet every need I'm aware of. I cannot exploit every opportunity. At times, I must prune away good, worthwhile branches to insure that the trunk and limbs are more prominent than the ever-expanding branches.

The goal of much that is written about life management is to enable us to do more in less time. But is this necessarily a desirable goal? Perhaps we need to get *less done,* but the right things.

When Mother Teresa received the Nobel Prize, a reporter asked a stinging question: "How can you receive this award when you've helped so few of the world's poor?" Mother Teresa replied that she couldn't accept responsibility for all the world's poor; she could only help those God asked her to be responsible for. We, too, can content ourselves with doing what God asks *us* to do.

Choices

Busyness isn't always the culprit. Even in slack times, we can be so preoccupied that God can't get our attention. Life becomes cluttered with too many options and competing interests. Decisive living requires the selective burning of bridges.

Annie Dillard, the Pulitzer-Prize-winning author, tells students that if they want to become writers, they must go at their lives with a broad axe. Vivid language, and true. To live with firm direction requires deliberate choices. Life is full of activities that consume time. Perhaps even some "must-do" activities need to be reevaluated.

Thoreau wrote, "I had three pieces of limestone on my desk, but I was terrified to find that they required to be dusted daily, when the furniture of my mind was all undusted still, and I threw them out of the window in disgust."[1]

Thoreau made a choice. So did Karen, a mother of three preschoolers. Although Karen enjoys sewing, she decided to put away her sewing machine and spend that time developing her relationship to God.

John Woolman, a godly tailor in the 1700s, became concerned that his flourishing tailoring business kept him from the things he believed God wanted him to do. Consequently, he referred some of his clients to competitors to give himself time to serve the Lord.

Perhaps unconsciously, we sometimes *choose* to complicate our life. We make decisions that actually hinder our progress toward our goals, instead of helping us.

Thoreau spoke to this idea: "However, if one designs to construct a dwelling house, it behooves him to exercise a little Yankee shrewdness, lest after all he find himself in a workhouse, a labyrinth without a clew, a museum, an almshouse, a prison, or a splendid mausoleum instead."[2]

A workhouse. Woman's work is never done. And judging from the list of projects I keep for my husband, man's work isn't either. However, the choices I make determine to some extent whether my home becomes a workhouse. If my standard is perfection, I'll never be finished. If I collect, there's more to dust.

A labyrinth without a clew. Mythology tells of Theseus who volunteered to be among those locked in the vast labyrinth beneath the city of Minos. Theseus faced two dangers underground: the fierce minotaur who devoured the poor souls trapped within, and the maze itself, an unending network of intricate tunnels. Before Theseus entered the tunnels, a beautiful princess stealthily slipped him a clew, a spool of thread. By unraveling the thread as he pursued the minotaur, Theseus laid a trail he hoped to retrace. Without the clew, Theseus would have wandered hopelessly through those winding passages.

A home becomes a threatening tangle of chambers without a thread to give continuity and purpose. A growing understanding of God's truth and a deepening commitment to obey it is the only worthy thread to follow.

A museum. A home can become primarily a place to display treasures. The focal point, the reason for its existence, is things—not people.

An almshouse. We can choose to buy a home that puts us in debt over our head. Instead of a refuge, our home becomes a stern taskmaster.

A prison. Some people are inmates in their own homes—afraid to leave lest someone break in, the petunias dry out, or the neighbor boy ride his bike on the lawn.

A splendid mausoleum. A home can become a tomb—a splendid, richly carved and overlaid place for the dead. We laugh sadly at stories of great Aunt Bertha who saved her prettiest dress to be buried in. But the same way of thinking can influence how we function in our home.

Values determine decisions. Thoreau said no to three pieces of limestone to say yes to developing himself. Life is full of choices. What will it cost me to keep my sewing projects, my flourishing tailoring business, my limestone? With eternity before us, let's not build "for this world a family mansion, and for the next a family tomb."[3]

Redefining success

Perhaps nothing diverts us from focused living more than our concept of success. Published studies inform us of what conveys power in body language, business lunches, and the cars we drive. We "dress for success." Society is not only preoccupied with the image of success, but for the most part is dependent on someone else to define success.

But what is success in God's sight?

When was Job most successful? Before hard times came and he still had his family, estate, and health intact? After God healed him and restored everything to him? Or was he more successful in his illness when he was still content with God? Was he successful when he perched on the edge of the sill most sorely tempted by his illness, yet didn't jump?

Was Jesus successful? He had no home of his own. The successful people of His day viewed Him skeptically, if not with hostility. His followers were a ragtag bunch without social or political influence. And even this motly crew fell away as He approached the Cross. None of His disciples accompanied Him in His darkest hour. He had neither wealth, political power, or unusual physical beauty.

Romano Guardini wrote, "How strange his life appears when measured by human standards. Nothing in it for such pat phrases as: he fought his way through to success; he blazed the way for his message and his mission; he ripened to maturity and fulfillment. . . . We begin to sense something of what takes place when God becomes not a classical hero, or overwhelming personality, or subduer of continents, but simply 'man'."[4]

Jesus measured His own success by one criterion: "I came . . . not to do my will but to do the will of him who sent me" (John 6:38). "I finished the work."

If we permit society to define success and fulfillment for us, we become sheep with a shepherd whose definition is 180 degrees from God's. The Christian must not possess an inner motivation based on image, status, possessions, or accomplishments, but rather on being faithful to what God has asked him to do. Refuse to accept the common definition of success and you may one day hear, "Well done, good and faithful servant" (Matthew 25:21).

Tensions

When I laid out my weekly schedule before God, I made Wednesday my study day. But every Wednesday interruptions invariably produced tensions. Should a visit from a nonChristian take precedence over scheduled events? Should I view interruptions as divinely appointed opportunities to serve, or as tests permitted to prove my obedience?

W. Glyn Evans said, "God must reserve for Himself the right of the initiative, the right to break into my life without question or explanation. That shattering phone call, that disturbing letter . . . may indeed be the first stage of God's interruption in my life. . . . Since God does the initiating, He must be responsible for the consequences."[5]

God is sovereign. He is in control. He alone knows the total program. He alone sees all the pieces. In Psalm 115:3 we read, "Our God is in heaven; he does whatever pleases him." A friend commented on this verse, "If what He's done pleases Him, it ought to please me, too."

But the issue here is not whether I will respond rightly to God's prerogative to impose unplanned items on my schedule and life. Rather, are these unplanned items necessarily meant to take priority over what is planned?

Suppose your family plans to attend a special musical performance. Ten minutes before you intend to leave, a lonely young man from your church drops by unexpectedly. You invite him in, and ask some general but personal questions, hoping that if he has come with a specific need he will open up. He says little, mostly small talk. Your children roll their eyes toward you imploringly. Their body language screams, "Look at the time! If we don't leave soon, it will be too late."

Your mind races. Why is it always so difficult to think clearly and objectively in these situations? What should you do? Is God overruling the family's plans with this visitor? Has this young man come with a special need? The music program is a sellout. You can't include him in your evening. Your family has anticipated this outing for two months. The children will be deeply disappointed if you don't go.

But suppose this young man is contemplating suicide, or giving his life to Christ? Possibly God led him to you to avert a tragedy or to share in his joy? Perhaps he was only out for a walk, saw your house, and dropped in for a brief visit.

The moment of decision is upon you. You must decide. Is there a right answer to this dilemma? Can you extract a principle that decides the question and eliminates the inner struggle? I don't think so.

Living the Christian life means living with tensions. The Christian experience does not come neatly packaged. Real Christianity cannot be lived by principles alone; real Christianity is lived in relationship to God. Even if we strive to live under God's direction and to make Him our audience, unplanned situations arise, complicating the neat pattern.

Jesus experienced interruptions too. A leper approached Jesus, fell at His feet, and begged, "Lord, if you are willing, you can make me clean" (Luke 5:12). Interruptions seldom come in such impassioned forms, but the question asked of us is the same: "If you are willing."

In this situation Jesus was willing. He touched the man, said, "Be clean," and healed him. Whatever Jesus was doing at the time—teaching, preaching, healing, talking, resting, praying, thinking, eating—He interrupted to redirect His energies.

Jesus ordered the man not to tell anyone, but to follow the laws prescribed for cleansing. "Yet the news about him spread all the more, so that crowds of people came to hear him and to be healed of their sicknesses. But Jesus often withdrew to lonely places and prayed" (Luke 5:15).

The key words for our consideration are *yet, but,* and *often. Yet* indicates that things didn't go as planned. Jesus told the leper not to tell anyone of his healing, *yet* the news spread and the crowds converged on Jesus. *But* indicates an effort exerted against the pervading pressures. Jesus didn't subject Himself to the whims of man. He didn't just flow with the tide. Unlike a leaf carried along by the water, Jesus made choices. Despite the opportunities for service, He chose to withdraw. *Often* indicates habit, custom, pattern. Jesus *often* withdrew to pray.

In my study of the Gospels, I find that Jesus did not respond positively to every interruption or suggested use of His time. How, then, did He determine which requests to fill, which to postpone, which to neglect completely? Isn't that the problem that causes us tension and frustration?

The answer, I believe, lies in the words *but* and *often.* Jesus chose often to pull away from the demands of life to pray, to refresh Himself, to get clear direction, and perhaps, to avoid further interruptions. That may be the reason that despite frequent interruptions, He moved through life decisively and without irritation.

Man shall not live by principles alone

How reassuring and comforting it would be to consign to the tensions of life a set of biblical principles and absolve ourselves of the struggle of personal responsibility. But even when the principles are clear, there is still the need to make personal application.

A young Christian from a Hindu family faced a dilemma. His neighbors considered him a disrespectful son because he no longer walked with his family to the marketplace to receive ashes on his forehead, and then return home to worship the family idols. He consulted with a mature Christian friend who asked him, "What are the principles involved?"

"I must worship the Lord alone. And I must honor my parents."

"That's right. Now spend time alone with the Lord to see how He wants you to apply them."

After prayer, the young Christian decided to walk with his parents to the marketplace, but when they worshiped the idols, he would step back and pray to the Lord.

Sometime later, another new Christian approached the young believer with the same problem. The Hindu Christian asked, "What are the principles involved?" He received the same answer from the new believer that he had given to his Christian friend months before. Then wisely he advised, "Get alone with God and see how He wants you to apply them."

How easy it would have been to prescribe his application of the principles. What a temptation to give the predigested answer. Instead, this young man encouraged his friend to apply the process that is absolutely essential for spiritual vitality. Each person must relate personally with Christ in applying His principles.

Jacques Ellul, a French law professor and lay theologian, writes, "At heart, this is a fight of faith: individual, and in the presence of God; and a living attitude, adopted according to the measure of faith of each person, and as the result of his or her faith. It is never a series of rules, of principles, or slogans, and every Christian is really responsible for his works and for his conscience."[6]

Biblical principles are not intended to resolve the tensions of life, or to eliminate the agonizing process of trying to live God-directed lives in a difficult situation or society. Principles cannot be applied as a recipe for righteousness. Jesus sternly chided the Pharisees for their careful adherence to man's interpretation of God's law. They meticulously conformed their lives to the formula—and they were spiritually dead.

Two of the most alive men who have ever lived were Jesus and John the Baptist. Both of these men lived deeply focused lives, characterized by devotion and self-discipline. They concerned themselves with what concerned God. Both stood fearlessly against the prevailing tide and cared little about material accumulation.

However, they lived their brief lives on earth very differently. John estranged himself from everyday life. Withdrawn from society, he lived a severely counter-culture lifestyle. Jesus, on the other hand, lived so thoroughly in His society that He was called "the son of Joseph." He ate and drank what everyone else ate and drank. Nothing in His appearance set Him apart. Jesus lived in the world, but was not of it. John lived on the fringe and charged, raving, into the world on forays.

Following a discussion of the differences of these two men, the Bible concludes, "But wisdom is proved right by all her children" (Luke 7:35). Jesus and John lived by biblical principles, but the outworking of those principles looked very different. Applications should not be identical.

J. H. Jowett, an English clergyman, wrote a prayer that expresses well the desire to live decisively under God's direction:

> Purify our souls, make our eyes keen and watchful, in order that we may discern Thy purpose at every turning of the way. Help us to hallow all our circumstances whether they appear friendly or adverse, and may we subdue them all to the King's will.[7]

Notes

1. Henry David Thoreau, *Walden and Other Writings* (New York: Bantam Books, 1962), page 132.
2. Thoreau, page 126.
3. Thoreau, page 133.
4. Romano Guardini, *The Lord* (Chicago: Henry Regnery Company, 1954), page 172.
5. W. Glyn Evans, as quoted in *Leadership*, vol. IV, no. 1, Winter 1983, page 111.

6. Jacques Ellul, *The Presence of the Kingdom* (New York: Seabury Press, 1967), page 20.
7. J. H. Jowett, *The Whole Armour of God* (London: Hodder and Stoughton, 1916), page 152.

4
How Busy Is Too Busy?

My shoulders drooped as I sat separated from my husband by a small table covered with our well-marked appointment calendars. Reviewing our calendars together always precipitated heart-felt communication. This night was no exception. When I complained about our busy schedules, Roger attempted to appease me by flipping the calendar forward two or three months to expose clean, bare pages. "I know this month is busy, but look at these months. They're light. Just hold on until we get through this month."

But the argument didn't pacify me this time. "The reason those months are bare is due to the fact that they are still several weeks away. By the time they get here, they will be as full as this one."

And I was right.

It isn't wrong to be busy. Serious involvement in promoting God's Kingdom requires activity. Jesus was busy—too busy to eat on one occasion (see Mark 3:20). He worked to the point of exhaustion on another occasion (see Mark 4:38). Read the book of Acts; Paul was busy. But a busyness that isn't God-directed and God-motivated is not God-blessed. Busyness can ravage the soul as thoroughly as idleness can.

Somehow the phrase *I'm busy* makes us feel secure. If we're busy, we must be important, perhaps even indispensable. Mistakenly, we equate busyness with production or contribution. The busiest people must be accomplishing the most. Or are they?

Toru Nagai, a Navigator staff man in Japan, wrote, "Whenever you ask a Japanese how he is doing, he almost always replies, 'Oh, I'm quite busy.' Even if he has nothing to do, his response is the same. Rest and relaxation in this culture are almost looked on as sin, so people stay busy, even if it is with activities of little importance. This tendency is so deeply rooted in the Japanese that it remains in many after they become Christians."

Like our Japanese friends, we may complain about the endless parade of demands facing us, but unconsciously we may have designed the lifestyle of hectic, unrelenting activity as protection.

Busyness can protect us

"Protect us from what?" you ask. Busyness may be our shelter from the hard, cold fact that our relationship with Christ has become perfunctory. We may live in an illusory world, remembering greener days without recognizing that our zeal has waned. But if we keep busy enough, the truth can't penetrate and expose our spiritual condition. Our visible, external life may be laudable, but our inner, spiritual life has shriveled.

Busyness may prevent us from facing a failing relationship—perhaps a troubled marriage. A couple can so pepper their lives with committee meetings, little league games, school activities, extra job responsibilities, church involvements, and craft classes that they never confront the uncomfortable void in their relationship as husband and wife. They complain about their schedules, but write in another activity to fill the few free hours on the calendar. Exhausted at the end of the day, they fall into bed too tired to discuss the issues screaming to be dealt with.

A busy life can be a shield from responsibility. A man may work overtime even when it isn't necessary, or cart home reams of papers in his briefcase and retreat from the family for the evening. The family may be made to feel sufficiently guilty if they protest about seeing so little of him. Afterall, he is busy working hard—not frivolously enjoying himself.

Mothers may heavily involve themselves outside the home if they find life at home frustrating. In Barbara Robinson's *The Best Christmas Pageant Ever,* the mother of the incorrigible and unruly Herdman children worked a double shift at the factory—but nobody blamed her. However, even when activities are worthwhile, to diligently occupy ourselves doing what we want, to keep from doing what we ought, is not commendable or wise.

If we appear busy, we make ourselves inaccessible and unavailable. Our obvious busyness keeps people at arm's length—and we are safe.

Busyness can prevent growth

Life in the fast-forward mode can prevent even spiritually sensitive people from getting the message. A young missionary couple was confined to bed for several months to recover from a serious illness. During that physically imposed cessation from activity, they learned much about themselves and each other that escaped their notice in the days of bustle.

The Bible mentions the purifying process by which impurities are removed from precious metal. As the metal is subjected to higher and higher temperatures, the impurities surface and are scooped off. Although pressures and trials expose the impurities in our life, they will settle to the bottom again unless we pause to acknowledge the imperfections and take time to act.

Busyness can hurt our work for God

We must scrutinize the rush of activities, because even venerable exertions may be keeping us from becoming and doing what God wants. A packed schedule may be detrimental not only to our life, but to those we seek to help.

A few years ago, I realized that our neighbors were drawn to us, but when we talked to them about the Lord their response was, "We couldn't be Christians; we couldn't live at your pace." They had been attracted to Christ in our lives, but the busyness in our lives scared them off.

In Exodus 18, Jethro, who was Moses' father-in-law, was appalled at the load Moses carried. From morning 'til evening Moses sat as judge while the masses lined up waiting their turn to air their problems and receive Moses' edict. As an outsider, Jethro perceptively concluded that the job was too heavy for one man. Moses and the people were wearing themselves out. Jethro advised Moses to do three things:

1. Be faithful to the responsibilities God gave him.
2. Redefine his responsibilities before God as the job got larger.
3. Delegate responsibility to capable, godly people.

This sterling strategy enabled Moses to withstand the strain, and better meet the needs of all the people.

The early Church faced a similar problem, recorded in Acts 6. As the number of disciples multiplied, the demands on the leaders expanded as well. When the Grecian Jews complained that their widows' needs were being overlooked, the Church leaders met to determine how best to fulfill their responsibility. They redefined their job: "It would not be right for us to neglect the ministry of the word of God in order to wait on tables." They also chose seven men to administrate the remaining tasks (Acts 6:2-4).

Beware the barrenness of too busy a life

After I shared some of these ideas with a small group of women in southern California, one woman aptly concluded, "We're often worst enemies to each other. When we see someone packing inordinate activities into her week, we sigh in admiration instead of asking, 'Why are you doing all this?'"

The Scriptures, too, prod us to thoughtful living: "Be very careful, then, how you live—not as unwise but as wise, making the most of every opportunity, because the days are evil. Therefore do not be foolish, but understand what the Lord's will is" (Ephesians 5:15-17).

These verses usually spur us to redouble our efforts, increase our speed, and expand our territory. However, three phrases from this portion should slow us down for reflection:

1. Be very careful, then, how you live—
2. Not as unwise but as wise,
3. Do not be foolish, but understand what the Lord's will is.

First, the Apostle Paul cautions us to give serious attention to how we live. Careful living requires thought. Earlier in his letter to the Ephesians, Paul tells us to become imitators of God, and live as children of light. It takes time to look for and at God so that we can be like Him.

Second, Paul tells us to live wisely. But how do we gain wisdom? James 1:5 comes to mind as nearly everyone's favorite verse on wisdom: "If any of you lacks wisdom, he should ask God, . . . and it will be given to him." Unfortunately, some people hold James 1:5 in reserve with the intention of setting it loose like a genie for their next crisis. God is gracious, and does sometimes intervene in catastrophes when his poor, ignorant people wail for help. We have all experienced this kind of help.

But this is not the pattern God has ordained for acquiring wisdom. In fact, Proverbs 1:23-33 teaches that if you have not made the pursuit of wisdom the direction of your life, God does not obligate Himself to run to your rescue. Proverbs is a wonderful book to study to gain insights on living wisely.

Third, we must understand what the Lord's will is so that we can make the most of every opportunity. The emphasis is not on learning to pack more into each day, so much as learning to order our day according to God's will. We must recover our time from wasteful activities, and liberate it for God's purposes. Again, reading the Bible and considering His truths are essential.

If you've identified yourself as too busy, step off that jet-propelled treadmill. Take some time to catch your breath and confront the condition of your soul, your relationships, and your work for God. Be very careful, then, how you live.

5
The Marrying of Service and Solitude

Throughout the ages, Christians have struggled to discern the proper balance between the cloistered existence and the life of reckless, zealous ministry—between bustling service and sacred hush—between Walden and the whirlwind. We contend with the Mary and Martha inside us. (Mary sat at Jesus' feet listening to what He said while her sister, Martha, was busy with the preparations for visitors in their home. (See Luke 10:38-42.)

To set aside everyday concerns and gaze uninterrupted at the Lord seems utopian and escapist. But the continual giving of ourselves in service for Christ brings a sobering awareness of our frail humanity and limited store. We become caught in the Mary-Martha dilemma, weighing the active life with the contemplative life.

True service for Christ, however, occurs only when Mary and Martha marry—when neither isolation or compulsion characterize our life. Bernard of Clairvaux, born in 1091, wrote, "Action and contemplation are very close companions; they live together in one house on equal terms; Martha is Mary's sister."[1] William Barclay also referred to a kind of coexistence: "The more one reads of the lives and works of great men, the more one sees that they have a twin capacity—the capacity to work and the capacity to wait."[2]

The Christian life should have a rhythm— doing and resting, speaking and listening, giving and receiving. The life of Jesus illustrates that perfect balance. This busy man (in perfect harmony with His Father, Himself, and His purpose on earth), who completed to the fullest the work given to Him, withdrew for prayer again and again. The Scriptures indicate that Jesus *worked* at getting alone, just as He worked at serving and teaching.

From the beginning of His ministry when He spent forty days alone in the desert, to the end of His ministry when He prayed nights on the Mount of Olives, Jesus' life was interlaced with periods of solitude. In these quiet times alone, He enjoyed a deep, abiding fellowship with His Father. Psalm 16:11 records David's expression of the exultant delight of this kind of communion with God: "You have made known to me the path of life; you will fill me with joy in your presence, with eternal pleasures at your right hand."

Jesus was ever occupied with relating to and pleasing the Father, not in making use of Him. Prayer was the expression of their unity, not a grip to wrest something from the Father. German pastor Otto Borchert wrote of their relationship, "Prayer went like a divine shuttle backwards and forwards between Him and the Father—speech and answer, giving and receiving, a continual loving aloud, in the most intimate tones that the world has ever heard."[3]

Jesus considered prayer crucial to ministry. Periods of prayer preceded the critical junctures of His life: before He began His public ministry, before choosing the twelve disciples, before His transfiguration that prepared His disciples for a fuller revelation of who He was, and before Gethsemane. On one occasion, He rebuked His disciples after they attempted, unsuccessfully, to cast out an evil spirit that had tormented a boy since his childhood. When the disciples asked why they were unable to drive it out, Jesus replied, "This kind can come out only by prayer" (Mark 9:29).

Solitude in the life of Jesus meant prayer, and prayer meant solitude. While the religious leaders stood conspicuously on street corners to pray, Jesus rose early in the morning or departed after dark to pray in private. It was His practice to enter His closet and shut the door.

Work is worship, also

To a culture that considered cloistered contemplation the highest status of the godly, Martin Luther proclaimed that work can be worship, too. Jesus said, "As long as it is day, we must do the work of him who sent me" (John 9:4). Jesus was a man of work, just as He was a man of prayer. Throughout the Gospels we see Him giving Himself to people: He healed, cast out demons, and proclaimed deepest truth. Jesus engaged in earnest conversation with those who knew little of serious talk. He demonstrated His servant disposition as He cooked meals for His disciples on the beach or washed their feet. His life was one of sacrificial service even apart from His death on the Cross. Virtue went from Him as He healed. His labors kept Him from food and brought Him to exhausted sleep in the stern of a boat. His ministry was hard work. Yet, as Romano Guardini has aptly observed, "Jesus is the bringer of the tidings of all tidings, but they neither crush nor drive him: he and his message are one."[4]

Jesus and His message are inseparable. He stands as the perfect embodiment of all He proclaimed and taught. His totally integrated life and ministry reflect His union with the Father. His work, the expression of His life, is worship.

The marrying of service and solitude is not to be found in the balance of a happy medium, or in a swath down the middle between service and solitude. Rather, it requires pursuing distinct paths in each direction. E. Stanley Jones, fifty years a missionary in India, said, "I found myself going off in solitude and reading my New Testament, and when I came across a verse that spoke of Him, I found myself reverently pressing my lips to that verse. . . . But I'm soon up on my feet again with a compulsion, a divine compulsion to share this with everyone, everywhere."[5]

This same rhythm of service and solitude characterized James Hervey (1713-1785): "But in-doors or out-of-doors, he was always full of his Master's business, always redeeming the time, always reading, writing, or speaking about Christ, and always behaving like a man who had recently come from his Lord's presence to say something, and was soon going back again."[6] Jesus, the Good Shepherd, says of His sheep, "He will come in and go out, and find pasture" (John 10:9). Jesus has called us to go out into the world for Him, but He has also called us to come to Him for refreshment.

Service and solitude each require our full attention. Neither can stand alone and be truly Christian. Service without time apart for spiritual nourishment, reflection, and fresh instruction from God deteriorates into humanitarian effort. True spiritual ministry acknowledges God as the source; the minister is merely the channel. The idea of living *in* Christ and letting Him live out His life in us is a recurring theme in the New Testament:

> No branch can bear fruit by itself; it must remain in the vine. Neither can you bear fruit unless you remain in me. I am the vine; you are the branches. If a man remains in me and I in him, he will bear much fruit; apart from me you can do nothing (John 15:4-5).

Not only must God minister *through* us, He

must minister *to* us. We must practice what we preach. Jesus called the honored teachers of His day whitewashed tombs because they taught what they didn't practice. Earlier He had declared, "Unless your righteousness surpasses that of the Pharisees and the teachers of the law, you will certainly not enter the kingdom of heaven" (Matthew 5:20). We must not become so busy serving that we fail to obey God ourselves.

Unless we take time to reflect on who God is (His attributes) and what He has done in the past (our history), and contemplate what He says He will do in the future (His promises), our good works may have no eternal substance. Service in His Kingdom consists not of isolated acts for the benefit of mankind, but of acts of obedience done for Him, in Him, because of who He is, and what He is like.

Likewise, solitude without service easily degenerates into self-absorption. Time with the Lord must quicken us to our needy world, not provide a soothing insulation from it. The natural fruit of looking at God is a heightened zeal and vigor to serve Him. As we ponder His grace and love, we long to express our gratitude in acts of obedience and to communicate Him to others.

If we emulate the Lord's pattern, we embrace the poles: service and solitude. We acknowledge that although the needs of the world are great and ever-present, we do no real service if we are spiritually destitute ourselves. Withdrawing to be alone is not indolence or dereliction of duty; it is an imperative. But we must also remember the Jesus who left His silent chamber to freely give His life for our sake thousands of times, and then faced the Cross.

Notes

1. Bernard of Clairvaux, *Selections from the Writings of Bernard of Clairvaux*, ed. Douglas V. Steere (Nashville, Tennessee: The Upper Room, 1961), page 25.
2. William Barclay, *Daily Celebration,* vol. II (Waco, Texas: Word Books, 1973), page 165.
3. Otto Borchert, *The Original Jesus* (London: Lutterworth Press, 1936), page 223.
4. Romano Guardini, *The Lord* (Chicago: The Henry Regnery Company, 1954), page 343.
5. E. Stanley Jones, *A Song of Ascents* (Nashville, Tennessee: Abingdon Press, 1968), page 29.
6. J. C. Ryle, *Christian Leaders of the 18th Century* (Edinburgh, Scotland: The Banner of Truth Trust, 1978), page 350.

6
Solitude

Have you ever stood ankle-deep in the ocean? Gradually, wave upon wave washes about your feet, rearranging and depositing sand. And if you stand there long enough, you will find not only your feet, but your legs also buried beneath the sand. You don't have to do anything. It is enough to do nothing.

It is the same in the Christian life. You don't have to do anything to sink into worldly patterns of thinking and living. The world system in which we live floods in, wave upon wave: respectable waves of religious legalism or finding favor through good works, or the more garish, neon-lighted waves of promised pleasure, waves of articulate intellectualism, waves of well-tailored, navy pinstriped success, and a continuous media wave of slim, chic, utterly charming lives portraying promiscuity, dishonesty, greed, and violence as funny, inevitable, and acceptable.

The waves of the world wash against us, sometimes gently, almost unnoticed. At other times the waves come with thundering force. And all the time, they heap their sediment around us.

The Church has not escaped the ravage of the waves. Statistics show that divorce is epidemic inside the Church as well as outside. Professing Christians cheat on income tax and in business dealings, engage in premarital and extramarital sex, and strive among themselves. Even many of the morally upright live shallow lives, not deep.

How easy it is to be sucked up by the current and find ourselves steadily drawn along the path of least resistance. Everything looks fine on the outside. We do the right things at the right times. We fit inconspicuously into our familiar culture: we know the language, when to say "Amen" (or to absolutely abstain, depending on the congregation), when to sit and stand as the church service progresses—but inside, perhaps even without our awareness, our spiritual vitality ebbs.

Our everyday environment seduces, taunts, and rages against the Christ-life within us. Without concentrated, deliberate action on our part to nourish our spiritual life, the oncoming tide wears away the undergirding foundation of our faith. To stanch the flow, to control the erosion, Christians must do more than hold our skirts higher. We must spend time apart with God. There is no growth in holiness apart from it.

But we live in a noisy, busy world. Silence and solitude are not twentieth-century words. They fit the era of Victorian lace, high-button shoes, and kerosene lamps better than our age of television, video arcades, and joggers wired with earphones. We have become a people with an aversion to quiet and an uneasiness with being alone.

Our practical, materialistic society so values action over meditation, study, and prayer that we often feel guilty when we stop to think, study, or pray. Even when we pause, we're still racing inside. The needs of the world press in on us. The opportunities for service scream in our ears. How can we withdraw from the vital mainstream of action when the needs are so great?

But even those who do withdraw to a quieter, purer life find it isn't a simple matter. Recluses with good intentions often fail to reach that longed-for, sublime simplicity. They cart along to Utopia their bedeviling neuroses, enslaving habits, and flawed character. They labor to strain off the external scum of life, but alas, they find that the internal scum remains. They strain at gnats and swallow camels. Within reside confusion, strife, dissatisfaction, and the hurts of life. They may experience aloneness without gaining any benefit of solitude.

Some seek solitude to escape the world's foulness and pollution, or to avoid the discomfort of relating to others. But for the Christian, the reason to pursue quiet aloneness is different. Christianity is a secret companionship. It is the only relationship in which I can be fully understood without speaking a word. My spirit communes with God even in total silence. Prayer is His provision for a degree of solitude even when I can't get away from it all. When my heart expresses itself to God, we are alone even in a crowd.

Thoreau's cabin at Walden Pond was not far from town. This location confirms that it is possible to experience solitude without being remote. Susannah Wesley, the mother of a large family, would flip her apron over her head as she sat praying in the midst of that busy household. That cotton apron didn't filter out the noise, but by that simple act, she crept away with God for refreshment and companionship.

God considers solitude very important to the development of spiritual leadership. He often imposed periods of solitude on His chosen leaders. Moses experienced forty years of isolation before God charged him to lead the people out of Egypt. God called him apart on other occasions throughout his life. David knew quiet, reflective times as a shepherd boy, and later, while in exile. The Psalms reveal him as a man who spent time alone with God.

Why solitude?

Christians are born complete in Christ, but not mature. We have in Him all we need for life and godliness. But the Christ-life is developed through a process of nourishment and exercise. Our faith must be fed and our obedience given opportunity to express itself. Time alone with God reveals who God is and what He wants done. Without a growing understanding of His ways and His will, we cannot trust and obey in spirit and in truth.

The Lord has warned us to beware of the world's conforming power on our life, and instead, to be transformed into Christ-likeness. If we remain inert, the world will steadily press in on us to batter, bully, coax, and delude, until we toe the line. So we must take the offensive in order that we be changed into God's image, not the world's. According to Romans 12:2, this process takes place by the renewing of our mind. In 2 Corinthians 3:18 we read that as we focus our gaze on Jesus, we will begin to reflect His glory. Transformation occurs by renewing and focusing. Both require time to assimilate the Word of God.

Solitude isn't a new idea. The first human couple walked and talked with their Creator in the Garden of Eden. At the heart of life, in all its intended fullness and perfection, man must commune with God. A growing communion with the Lord is the goal of solitude.

Like nonChristians, Christians must exercise, eat a balanced diet, and get fresh air and proper rest if they are to contribute to their good health. In addition, Christians have a secret inner life that must be cared for. Christianity is not an ascetic religion that strips the material world of value, but God does say that what a man is *inside* is more important than his outward appearance, economic status, or position in society. God looks at the heart (see 1 Samuel 16:7). Christ directed His most stinging rebukes to the Pharisees, who neglected their inner life but diligently exercised outward forms to give a spiritual impression.

What solitude does for you

Essential to the focused life is our commitment to God above all else. This commitment cannot be sustained unless we spend time with Him to know and understand Him. The Lord declared through Jeremiah that this is our worthiest pursuit:

> Let not the wise man boast of his wisdom or the strong man boast of his strength or the rich man boast of his riches, but let him who boasts boast about this: that he understands and knows me, that I am the Lord, who exercises kindness, justice and righteousness on earth, for in these I delight (Jeremiah 9:23-24).

Time alone with the Lord cleanses the mind. Jim Downing, a Navigator staff man, says that even when no particular thought or blessing emerges from his Bible reading, the water of the Word running through his mind has a purifying effect.

Focusing on God helps us view this present, illusory world with perspective by setting it in eternity, and enables us to evaluate our current direction, desires, and plans. A Godward gaze often exposes error or shame in our life.

Your choice

Thomas R. Kelly wrote, "If you say you haven't the time to go down into the recreating silences, I can only say to you, 'Then you don't *really* want to, you don't yet love God above all else in the world, with all your heart and soul and mind and strength.' For, except for spells of sickness in the family when the children are small, when terrific pressure comes upon us, we find time for what we *really want* to do."[1] J. Oswald Sanders summed up that thought when he said that we know God as well as we choose to. Arrange your life to accommodate Him.

Man's effort or God's blessing

How is the spiritual life formed within us? Is it a matter of discipline and persistent effort, or is it a gift from God totally apart from self-effort? Two back-to-back accounts in 2 Kings illustrate what I believe is the right perspective.

After the death of Ahab, king of Israel, Mesha, king of Moab, refused to continue supplying Israel with lambs and wool. Joram, Israel's new king, enlisted the help of Jehoshaphat, king of Judah, and set out to teach Mesha a lesson. Enroute to Moab through the desert of Edom, the two armies found themselves without water. Jehoshaphat suggested they inquire of the Lord. The word of the Lord, spoken by the prophet Elisha, was, "Make this valley full of ditches. For this is what the Lord says: You will see neither wind nor rain, yet this valley will be filled with water, and you, your cattle and your other animals will drink" (2 Kings 3:16-17).

The second incident involved a widow in dire straits. Her deceased husband's creditors threatened to take her two sons into slavery unless she could pay off the debt, but all she had left was a little oil. The prophet Elisha told her to collect as many jars as possible from neighbors, retreat behind closed doors with her boys, and pour the oil into the jars. Miraculously, her limited supply of oil was unlimited until the last jar was full. She sold the oil to pay the debt.

Ditches and jars—receptacles that needed to be filled. Both incidents required some effort from people, but always with the knowledge that God must do the filling. God has both commanded us to seek Him, and promised to reveal Himself when we do.

Paul challenged the young pastor, Timothy, to train himself in godliness (see 1 Timothy 4:7). Paraphrased, Paul might have said, "Timothy, take responsibility for your spiritual condition. The world system you must live in will not provide what is needed for you to develop in your faith, and you cannot depend on the religious community. Schedule time for training, set your mind on the goal, discipline yourself to work at it. You must make your own environment for growth."

Our society has become very dependent on external motivation to precipitate change or learning. We think we must attend seminars and classes, and if the schedule conflicts or money is short, we excuse ourselves for not learning or growing. But a disciple is a learner. God is our teacher. He has given the Holy Spirit to indwell and tutor us. We need not depend on organized resources and experts to stimulate and nurture our spiritual life. Pray for help. Seek help. Search out people who can help establish you in your relationship with God, for He does indeed use people. But if help is not forthcoming, God will assist you as you train yourself in godliness.

Develop spiritual disciplines

Henri J.M. Nouwen, pastor and teacher, wrote, "Precisely because our secular milieu offers us so few spiritual disciplines, we have to develop our own. We have, indeed, to fashion our own desert where we can withdraw every day, shake off our compulsions, and dwell in the gentle healing presence of our Lord."[2]

After a time of family feasting, it was Job's regular custom to rise early in the morning and sacrifice a burnt offering for each of his children out of concern for their relationship to the Lord (see Job 1:5). Daniel prayed three times a day (see Daniel 6:10-13). For years, my friend Joniva Mondragon, a missionary in Korea, has fasted on Sundays and spent the afternoon in Bible reading, prayer, and correspondence.

The Lord retreated for prayer daily: "Each day Jesus was teaching at the temple, and each evening he went out to spend the night on the hill called the Mount of Olives, and his disciples followed him" (Luke 22:39).

What established routines and choices give form to your life? Carefully cultivated habits that grow out of a spiritually developed value system have great importance. Francois Fenelon advised, "You will do well so to regulate your time that you may have every day a little leisure for reading, meditation, and prayer, to review your defects, to study your duties, and to hold communion with God. You will be happy when a true love to Him shall make this duty easy."[3]

Persistence

God blesses persistence. As a result of his persistence, Jacob's name was changed to Israel (see Genesis 32:24-30). The Greek woman born in Syrian Phoenicia was not easily turned aside. When Jesus failed to respond to her request to exorcise the demon from her daughter, this woman tenaciously persuaded Him to do so (see Mark 7:24-30). Jesus also taught the value of persistent prayer in the parable of the widow and the unjust judge.

God does not respond to persistence because we have managed to wrest His blessing from Him, or have convinced Him that we are unworthily worthy, or have annoyed Him to the point that He succumbs to our demands. God responds to persistence because it communicates earnestness and singular desire. Those who care less fervently are more easily diverted and dissauded from the pursuit of God Himself. The Lord has promised, "You will seek me and find me when you seek me with all your heart" (Jeremiah 29:13). Our God is sovereign. He gives spiritual gifts, provisions, and even the knowledge of Himself as He chooses. He can reveal Himself to anyone He chooses, but He has pledged Himself to those who seek Him with all their heart.

Listening

"We have the use of a sailboat and find joy in seeing how the wishes of men and winds have to work together. It is good to bow before the forces of nature as well as to conquer them. The spirit of our time lays such strong emphasis on the conquering, the activity; I find that we also learn from listening, waiting, helpless expectancy."[4]

Listening, waiting, helpless expectancy. What does it mean for the Christian to submit to the Divine wind in his life? As I sit on the deck, the wind rushes through the leaves of our trees, rustling them, and then vanishes unseen, leaving them still and quiet. I am sometimes conscious and sometimes oblivious to the wind's work. (I am more aware as it flips the pages I'm working on.) An airplane overhead drowns out the wind's gentler tones; birds enhance it; my thoughts concentrated elsewhere overrule it, until I realize its vengeance has scattered the contents of my folder across the deck.

Unfortunately, God sometimes has to blow through my life like a raging typhoon before He gets my attention. My focus is elsewhere—on God's work or the concerns of this life—and I fail to hear His voice in the wind. The frantic pace can carry over into our devotional times. We dash into God's presence, hurriedly read a Scripture passage, whip through our prayer list, ask His advice, but rush off before He speaks.

Missionary statesman and author J. Oswald Sanders set aside his evenings for two weeks when faced with a critical decision. Each evening he read the Bible and prayed regarding the opportunity confronting him. During this period of reading, praying, and listening for God's direction, a clear course of action emerged. If we are to hear God speak, we need not have a silent environment, but we must have a quiet heart.

Like Samuel in 1 Samuel 2, sometimes when stirred we jump up to serve, unaware that the Lord called, not to jolt us into action, but to get our attention. To quell the uneasiness we redouble our efforts, when all the while, He called because He has something to tell us.

No relationship escapes erosion. The tides of time and the cares of this world do their work silently, without fanfare, without our invitation or permission. Only great watchfulness and care can sandbag the vulnerable coastline. For a Christian, solitude is not an escape from the difficulties of life, or a period of mental stupor and lethargy. It is a time for alertness and expectancy, a time to promote and sustain our life in Christ, because it will not flourish without times of solitude.

Notes

1. Thomas R. Kelly, *A Testament of Devotion*, ed. Douglas V. Steere (Nashville, Tennessee: The Upper Room, 1955), page 16.
2. Henri J.M. Nouwen, *The Way of the Heart* (New York: Ballantine Books, 1981), page 17.
3. Francois Fenelon, *Selections from the Writings of Francois Fenelon*, ed. Thomas S. Kepler (Nashville, Tennessee: The Upper Room, 1962), page 9.
4. Kelly, page 7.

7
Service

In Christianity, service and solitude are inseparable. God's Kingdom is best advanced when they
are joined—each stimulating the other to new
depths. Walden becomes a stagnant pond without
the outflow of service. And serving apart from still
moments listening to and drawing strength from
God produces a destructive, continual whirlwind.
Although service and solitude may be thought of
as separate poles in the Christian experience, they
are the aggregate of God's intention. Like solitude, service is essential to spiritual health.

But how shall we define service?

Let's look at Jesus' concept of service. Isaiah
61 foretold the Messiah's ministry of healing and
freeing those in bondage. Jesus fulfilled those

prophetic words as He moved among men as a merciful and compassionate restorer, healer, and liberator. But His mission was not to eradicate the pain of illness or poverty. He never healed everyone or overthrew unjust social structures to even out the inequalities of society. Jesus viewed the needs of men—their infirmities, bondage, and poverty—as portals through which deeper eternal needs might be met. Good works were not the ministry; they were the soothing balm and massive chain cutters that ministered to man's immediate needs that they might look to God for their greater need. The critical issue was that man must come to faith in God through Christ.

Jesus viewed all of life as an opportunity to reveal the Father and to display His glory. When His disciples asked whose sin caused a man to be born blind, Jesus redirected their focus. The important thing was not to sniff out the cause and affix blame for the problem, but to see that this unfortunate situation could showcase God's power and goodness (see John 9:1-3).

Throughout the ages, God's concern has been "that they might know that I am the Lord." The word *they* in that statement extended beyond the Jews to the world. God drew Israel to His breast that they might be used to communicate who He is to the nations.

Jesus' intimate conversation with the Father in John 17 gives penetrating insight into Jesus' view of His ministry on earth. He came to glorify the Father by completing the work He was sent to do. His assignment was to make the Father known to us. In living among us, He did just that. The Bible tells us that He is the image of the invisible God, the radiance of God's glory, and the exact representation of His being. His character and personality reveal the Father; so do His works.

The works and teachings of Jesus make known God's intent and Word. All Jesus said and did was in order that we might know the Father, which He defined as eternal life. The Gospels record sermons, parables, and conversations in which Jesus presented ultimate truth. He spoke with an urgency about spiritual realities as He proclaimed the Father's words to us that man might be saved. And His supreme work on the Cross made provision for that redemption.

However, Jesus' prayer in John 17 reveals His mission to not only *save* us, but also to *send* us. He protected His own from the Enemy and nurtured them with greatest fervor, because He intended to leave them behind. Just as Jesus set Himself apart to fully do the Father's will, He prayed that His people would be set apart, or sanctified, for His purposes: "As you sent me into the world, I have sent them into the world" (John 17:18). Jesus was sent to reveal the Father in His character, words, and works. That is our mission as well.

Jesus' service was God-inspired, God-motivated, God-empowered. Just as His service expressed His union with the Father, Jesus intends that our life reflect our union with Him.

Serving from my union with Christ

Serving God through my own resources is religion; serving man through my own resources is humanitarian effort. But Christian service is something else again. Like religion and humanitarian effort, Christian service requires man's efforts. In fact, the cost may be great. But the real work comes from the power of Another's life within. Christ indwells every believer and longs to impact the world as He lives out His life in His host. The Christian is the flesh of Christ to His world. Christian service is not man's attempt to imitate his Lord's life, but an expression of the reality of it within. The Scriptures call it a mystery: "Christ in you, the hope of glory" (Colossians 1:27).

This union defies packaging. No one can explain its working. It is a mystery. Galatians 2:20 (KJV) contains a statement and counter-statement that must be held in tension: "I am crucified with Christ: nevertheless I live." I'm dead. I'm alive. "Yet not I, but Christ liveth in me: and the life which I now live in the flesh I live by the faith of the Son of God, who loved me, and gave himself for me."

Although the power comes from Christ within, our part is not to become a lifeless blob, a mere shell, or a soggy vegetable. Our will and energy are essential elements of our union with Christ. The Bible is sprinkled lavishly with admonishments to *press* towards the mark, *run* the race, and *fight* the good fight. The mystery of the union is misunderstood as much by those who say, "Lord, You do it all through me"—and let every muscle go limp—as it is by those who labor in their own strength. A mystery.

A look at the Servant

A discussion of service must consider the server, or as the Bible calls him, "the servant." Throughout the ages, God has referred to His faithful people as His servants. The Bible even calls Jesus "His holy Servant."

And truly Jesus came as a servant of God and men. He unflinchingly carried out the Father's will:

> Sacrifice and offering you did not desire, but a body you prepared for me; with burnt offerings and sin offerings you were not pleased. Then I said, "Here I am—it is written about me in the scroll—I have come to do your will, O God" (Hebrews 10:5-7).

Unlike the religious leaders who exercised unquestioning authority over the people, Jesus came not as a ruler, but as a servant. From the example of His own life He teaches, "Whoever wants to become great among you must be your servant, and whoever wants to be first must be slave of all. For even the Son of Man did not come to be served, but to serve, and to give his life as a ransom for many" (Mark 10:43-45).

He ransomed us that we, too, might serve God and man. Like Jesus, for whom the Father prepared a body that He might become the acceptable sacrifice for sin, we are called to present our bodies to God as "living sacrifices," to say, "Here I am—I have come to do your will."

The desire to serve God and man lives in

every true believer; it is the supernatural result of our faith. We may expect works of righteousness to accompany our belief in Christ, for James has said, "Faith without deeds is dead" (James 2:26).

But in our ardor to serve, we often overlook a critical truth: *The servant doesn't choose his task.* Our concept of serving God may be doing what we would like to do—for God. We tell God what we'll do for Him, and what we won't do; where we'll go for Him, and where we won't go. We even tell Him what mustn't interfere with our plans to serve Him. We pray, "Lord, help Sharon get well before this weekend. How can I serve You if You don't eliminate this problem?"

Prayers like these must seem ludicrous to God. He is the Master. The Master assigns the task. And if our Master wants to assign the care of a sick child instead of leading a Bible study, that's His prerogative. George MacDonald, a Scottish pastor and novelist, said,

> No man can order his life, for it comes flowing over him from behind. . . . The one secret of life and development is not to devise and plan but to fall in with the forces at work—to do every moment's duty aright—that being the part in the process allotted to us: and let come—not what will, for there is no such thing—but what the eternal thought wills for each of us, has intended in each of us from the first.[1]

The Scriptures, indeed, teach that God has a plan for our life. In 2 Corinthians 5:15 we read that the regenerate heart is not at liberty to live for itself because Christ "died for all, that those who live should no longer live for themselves but for him who died for them and was raised again." God has some service in mind for each of us, "for we are God's workmanship, created in Christ Jesus to do good works, which God prepared in advance for us to do" (Ephesians 2:10). Our part is to give ourselves to Him, accepting the assignment He bestows.

A servant is not free to serve on his own terms. Jesus said, "You did not choose me, but I chose you to go and bear fruit" (John 15:16). So, we have been chosen to "run with perseverance the race marked out for us" (Hebrews 12:1). The race set before us may not be on the track we'd choose. Joni Eareckson Tada would not have chosen to minister from a wheelchair, nor would the great hymnwriter Fanny Crosby have chosen to run her race in total darkness. Perhaps we would not choose the people God has placed around us, or the location or circumstances we find ourself in, but a servant is not above his Master. Let us fix our eyes on Jesus who faithfully ran His race—enduring the Cross and despising the shame.

A Servant is not above his Master

"A student is not above his teacher, nor a servant above his master. It is enough for the student to be like his teacher, and the servant like his master" (Matthew 10:24-25). This verse could easily form the basis for a lifetime of study and meditation.

Certainly, to contemplate the life and service of our Teacher and Master would be a bottomless treasure store. But this verse also stands as a warning and a standard. As His servants, we should not expect better treatment at the hands of men than He received. He came to give His life.

Sacrifice is an integral part of the Christian life. Christ's act of obedience on the Cross points the way for us. But that one-time act is only part of the story. His entire life was one act of sacrifice after another. He became flesh and dwelt among us. Jesus took a giant step of sacrifice for us—from glory to a stable, from the vastness of eternity to the confinement of Nazareth: "For you know the grace of our Lord Jesus Christ, that though he was rich, yet for your sakes he became poor, so that you through his poverty might become rich" (2 Corinthians 8:9). "Who, being in very nature God, did not consider equality with God something to be grasped, but made himself nothing, taking the very nature of a servant, being made in human likeness" (Philippians 2:6-7).

Life could have been so different for Him if He had used His power to make Himself more comfortable. All power in Heaven and earth belonged to Him; He could have spoken into existence a clean, quiet, warm place for His birth or a home of His own for His adult life. But He made His first cry as a man-child from a cave-like stable and enjoyed the homes of others, never having one of His own. He didn't use His power to miraculously supply water when thirsty; He asked a hated Samaritan woman for a drink. He knew hunger, fatigue, and struggle. He could have had twelve legions of angels as personal bodyguards, but instead He surrounded Himself with twelve *very human* disciples.

The Lord will not overlook our needs, but He will allow us to demonstrate our love and commitment through acts that cost us something. Frederick Buechner, a novelist, wrote, "To sacrifice something is to make it holy by giving it away for love."[2]

What service does God ask of us?

The essence of our service

When asked, "What must we do to do the works God requires?" Jesus responded, "The work of God is this: to believe in the one he has sent" (John 6:28-29). Faith in Christ. That is where the Christian life begins, and by faith it continues. A key verse for the entire span of Scripture states, "The righteous will live by faith" (Galatians 3:11).

By faith we became God's children, but that faith is always incomplete, though sincere. Throughout life, the Christian's work is to grow in the knowledge of God, that our faith might be established, firm, and mature. A Christian thinker from the Reformation era said, "I am forced to the conclusion that a man has as much faith as he has personal knowledge of God in Christ." To this end, Paul prayed for the Ephesian believers "that the God of our Lord Jesus Christ, the glorious Father, may give you the Spirit of wisdom and revelation, so that you may know him better" (Ephesians 1:17).

Unlike academic pursuits, the knowledge of God cannot be gained through intellectual channels alone. It is a knowledge that must be experienced. Our will and body must assent as well as our mind.

An example of this process: the Bible states that faith comes by hearing the Word of God. God's words are spirit and life, and demand a response. James concurs: "Do not merely listen to the word, and so deceive yourselves. Do what it says" (James 1:22). When we choose to do God's will, we become more convinced that the words of Scripture come from Him, and that He will reveal more of Himself to us who obey, as promised. Both outcomes strengthen our faith.

The essence of our work for God is to *believe in Christ* and to *obey Him as Lord.* In true biblical faith, these cannot be divorced as separate entities. They are unalterably wedded. As we grasp more fully who Christ is and what He wants from us, we must make choices in our thinking and actions that harmonize with His character and purposes. These choices encompass the full spectrum of life. It is in living under the lordship of Christ that the secular can become spiritual and the seemingly insignificant moment can become a sacrament.

The scope of our service

There is no experience that begins to match the scope of Christian service. Only the lack of faith, vision, and obedience can restrict our impact.

Christian servants must have a *telescopic* view. Stop watching your own feet. Lift up your eyes. Look left and right. Widen your vision. Fix your eyes beyond the horizon. Why? Because the concern of God reaches to the uttermost part of the world—every creature, tongue, tribe, people. The eye of God looks on the masses with compassion because they are like harassed and helpless sheep without a shepherd to care for them. He cares that they have not heard the good news that can liberate them from the kingdom of darkness. This concern is expressed in Jesus' last words to His disciples before He was translated into Heaven: "Therefore, go and make disciples of all nations" (Matthew 28:19).

Matthew 24:14 underlines the urgency of the task: "And this gospel of the kingdom will be preached in the whole world as a testimony to all nations, and then the end will come." Jesus says that all the world must be represented in Heaven before He will set up His Kingdom on earth. Not one language, tribal group, or color will be absent. We cannot say, "Even so, come quickly," unless we take the task of world evangelization seriously. The assignment He left with the first-century Christians has never been revoked or ammended. Our work has been defined: evangelize the world.

We must not fail to obey this Great Commission. We must go ourselves or send others. We can pray for more laborers to go and for those already laboring. We can financially support those who go. For "how, then, can they call on the one they have not believed in? And how can they believe in the one of whom they have not heard? And how can they hear without someone preaching to them? And how can they preach unless they are sent? As it is written, 'How beautiful are the feet of those who bring good news!'" (Romans 10:14-15).

To the fervent young missionary, it must have seemed God was working against him. J. Oswald Smith's heart burned for missions, but one overseas assignment after another resulted in his being sent home because of illness. How unreconcilable that the God who yearns for the world to hear the gospel, and who has within Him power to heal, would thwart the effort of one zealous to go.

But God assigned another area of service. Smith became the pastor of the People's Church of Toronto, Canada, a church that in the 1950s gave $282,000 in one year to missions. During this same time, Dr. Smith helped a church in Boston, whose mission budget was $3,200 a year, hold a yearly mission conference. Within six years, the church's budget for missions rose to over $200,000. Would J. Oswald Smith's impact have been greater had he gone himself?

God expects a telescopic vision that involves us in world evangelization, but He assigns us our part. It may mean making quilts for Christian relief agencies to distribute to earthquake victims, going to the mission field for a month or two to share a needed skill (like dentistry, carpentry, or computer programming), or handling the printing and mailing of a missionary's prayer letter. It does mean prayer, giving, and a willingness to go.

We must also develop a *bifocal* view, involving ourselves in the propagation of the gospel without neglecting to serve where we are. Jesus said, "You will be my witnesses in Jerusalem, and in all Judea and Samaria, and to the ends of the earth" (Acts 1:8). A concern for the world doesn't nullify the need to minister where we are; we must serve in "Jerusalem" without losing sight of the world.

Christians of every era must serve their generation that people might know who Jesus is, believe in Him, and obey Him. Our job is to "make men conscious of the stupendous reality knocking at their doors"[3] and the terrible consequences of refusing to respond.

How is this done?

God's method is through the preaching of the Scriptures. God honors the proclamation of His Word, both verbally and non-verbally. Man must be instructed in the truth, but learns more from pattern than from precept. We dare not neglect the potent influence of goodness for the cause of Christ.

Goodness is a powerful magnet. British author C. S. Lewis said that through reading the works of the Scottish clergyman George MacDonald, he began to love goodness. Lewis considered this to be the priming that prepared him to come to Christ. This should not surprise us. Romans 2:4 reminds us that God's goodness to man should lead him to repentance. Our good works draw people to Christ as well.

In *What's Mine's Mine,* George MacDonald hits on a detriment to personal goodness: "She sometimes wished she were good; but there are thousands of wandering ghosts who would be good if they might without taking the trouble; the kind of goodness they desire would not be worth the life to hold it."[4]

But we may be sure that goodness is worth the effort because God has redeemed us to do good. Titus 2:14 confirms this call: "Jesus Christ . . . gave himself for us to redeem us from all wickedness and to purify for himself a people that are his very own, eager to do what is good."

The Book of Titus praises goodness. Throughout the Epistle, Paul stirs God's people to love what is good, to devote themselves to doing what is good, and to teach what is good. Goodness should characterize our life, because our Lord "went around doing good" (Acts 10:38). Our good works are a powerful expression of Christ's life in us.

Good works are like a mixed bouquet of wild and cultivated flowers—profuse in their variety of form, color, and fragrance. The disciples chided the woman in Bethany for pouring expensive perfume on Jesus' head, but He said, "She has done a beautiful thing to me" (Matthew 26:10). Paraphrased, He might have said, "She has performed a beautiful *good work* upon me."

Dorcas sewed clothes for the needy. Cornelius gave money to the poor. The church cared for orphans and widows. Special offerings were taken for famine victims. Bringing up children is listed in the Bible as a good work. It is not difficult to add to the list: listening to someone who needs to talk, delivering a meal to an elderly person, volunteering to do laundry for a new mother, buying groceries for a neighbor with a broken leg, helping a widow change screens to storm windows. Many good deeds seem as common and unexciting as dandelions, and we may mistakenly discount their worth and impact. But small acts of kindness may, surprisingly, change from ragweed to orchids before our eyes.

In Matthew 25, God's people were stunned to realize that when they carried a pitcher of lemonade out to the neighborhood kids playing in the backyard, or helped an elderly man find the bus stop, or came to the aid of a motorist with a dead battery—they had done it for Jesus. A glass of water, a visit to a shut-in, a note of encouragement to your pastor or child's teacher—these dandelions are received as orchids.

> Then the King will say to those on his right, "Come, you who are blessed by my Father; take your inheritance, the kingdom prepared for you since the creation of the world. For I was hungry and you gave me something to eat, I was thirsty and you gave me something to drink, I was a stranger and you invited me in, I needed clothes and you clothed me, I was sick and you looked after me, I was in prison and you came to visit me."
>
> Then the righteous will answer him, "Lord, when did we see you hungry and feed you, or thirsty and give you something to drink? When did we see you a stranger and invite you in, or needing clothes and clothe you? When did we see you sick or in prison and go to visit you?"
>
> The King will reply, "I tell you the truth,

whatever you did for one of the least of these brothers of mine, you did for me" (Matthew 25:34-40).

Goodness is a powerful influence for the gospel. But alone it is insufficient. Edith Schaeffer tells in her book *Hidden Art* that early in her marriage, when vagrants came to her door for food, she would have them sit on the back porch while she carefully prepared a tray for them, arranging the food artistically and adding a garnish. These men from the dirty boxcars would receive the tray incredulously. Why would a stranger take such trouble for a tramp? The Gospel of John beside the hot soup and cookies gave a clue: this was a Christian lady. The answer had something to do with God and His love.

Openly identify with Christ.

C.T. Venugopal called clerks and higher officials together when he became a top official with India's government-run railroad and said, "I'm a Christian, but I want you to help me be a better one. If you see me depart from the high standards of Christianity, you come and tell me about it—it will help me."[5]

Later, Mr. Venugopal was sent to Pakistan to recover railroad records after the partition of Pakistan and India. His government instructed him to give one record for one record. But Mr. Venugopal, a hated Hindu entering a hostile Muslim country, came as a Christian giving them all their records—with no strings attached. The Muslims stood aghast and then retreated to discuss the situation. They returned, giving Mr. Venugopal all his country's records.

His presence among them made such an impact, that when they asked him how much their country owed India, they took Mr. Venugopal's word, and refused to check the records.

Later, when Burma gained her independence, she sent a request: "Please send us the services of Venugopal to straighten out relations in the Burma railway. We want Venugopal and no other."[6]

Christian service has a *microscopic* aspect as well. This service may be nearly invisible to the naked eye. Hidden and minute, it often not only escapes others' notice, but the servant himself may fail to recognize his service. In fact, it may appear to be the very essence of frustration and a hindrance to our service for God.

The acid test of Christianity is not giving our life at the stake or in the lion's den, but giving it little by little, day after day, moment by moment, a drop at a time, in the common duties of life assigned to us. These tasks seem too small in themselves to have any significance, but their cumulative effect keeps us from pursuing more "noble endeavors." Frustration grows as we feel our options shrinking, our life drained away by the mundane.

But it is not the job that determines its worth and impact, rather the heart of the person approaching and executing the task. No work in itself is spiritual or secular. Prayer can be secular if it is offered as a perfunctory exercise of form; sorting socks or changing the oil can become a sacrament when done with a pure heart surrendered to God. The motive of the heart either degrades or hallows all work. Scottish pastor John Caird, in a sermon preached before the Queen in 1855, said, "Religion consists, not so much in doing spiritual or sacred acts, as in doing secular acts from a sacred or religious motive."[7]

God gave unfathomable dignity to common labor when He made His only begotten Son a carpenter, not a king or a scholar. Our Lord's dear mother, even after giving birth to God in flesh (the most awesome event in human history), still baked bread, washed clothes, and did the dishes. Christ made a fire and cooked an early-morning breakfast for His disciples *after* His resurrection. God's order is not to abolish the mundane and routine from the life of the Christian, but to transform it.

Because Christ lives in us, all our work can be spiritual work. He elevates all He touches, turning the distasteful job into a holy act of service. His life infuses us, demanding expression. Even in the ordinary duties of life, He will reveal Himself. The tiniest, most nearly invisible labors are not lost to the cause of Christ. First Timothy 5:25 teaches, "Good deeds are obvious, and even those that are not cannot be hidden." The impact of our work cannot be suppressed.

Neither can our service be nullified by adverse circumstances. Remember Paul, who saw his imprisonment as a means of furthering the gospel. The persecution of the early Church did not quench the movement; it spread it. Famine and earthquake have provided entrance for the gospel on the wings of Christian relief in countries closed to missionaries. Five young men were murdered in Ecuador by the tribesmen they sought to reach. But instead of snuffing out the missionary effort, the murders stimulated it. Prayers and giving increased. Others volunteered to go. Victory swallowed defeat.

Apparent hindrances in our life can become vehicles to promote God's purposes. His work is supernatural. He can work through anything. Abigail would not have chosen to be married to a fool; Zachariah and Elizabeth would not have chosen to be childless for many years. But we are servants; servants do not choose their service.

The whirlwind

Serving God can be a whirlwind. It was in Jesus' ministry; it can be today. After the Twelve had completed their first official ministry assignment, they returned to report the outcome to Jesus. They were excited, but also in need of rest. Yet, many people pressed around them: "They did not even have a chance to eat" (Mark 6:31). Recognizing their need, Jesus drew them away to a solitary place for some rest. But the whirlwind did not dissipate. The crowds anticipated their vacation spot and met them there. Jesus was moved with compassion for the people and preached to them. He pressed the disciples into service, feeding the people and picking up the leftovers. Then immediately, Jesus sent the disciples to the boat, to cross back to the other side of the lake. They strained at the oars in a strong wind until Jesus calmed it. They finally arrived safely on the shore—only to be met by another crowd. Everywhere they went, people flooded to Jesus.

The whirlwind is often a healthy part of following after Jesus. Certainly, a life constantly characterized by the whirlwind would indicate a problem, but a life never caught in the rush and press of activity would suggest a focus on self-preservation. Jesus said if we seek to save our life, we will lose it (Matthew 10:39). It is a necessary expression of the Christ-life to spend for the cause—beyond the point of comfort.

Notes
  1. *George MacDonald: An Anthology*, ed. C.S. Lewis (New York: MacMillan Company, 1947), pages 134-135.
  2. Frederick Buechner, *Wishful Thinking* (New York: Harper and Row, 1973), page 83.
  3. Romano Guardini, *The Lord* (Chicago: The Henry Regnery Company, 1954), page 343.
  4. *George MacDonald: An Anthology*, page 142.
  5. E. Stanley Jones, *A Song of Ascents* (Nashville, Tennessee: Abingdon Press, 1968), page 118.
  6. Jones, page 120.
  7. Grenville Kleiser, comp., *The World's Great Sermons*, vol. VI (London: Funk and Wagnalls, 1908), pages 171-172.

8
Contentment

Suppose someone said, "I am ready for anything and equal to everything. Bring on life." Would you be incredulous? I might say, "Give them time. Life will shatter their illusion and give them a taste of reality and a saner view. These are obviously the sentiments of someone young and sheltered, someone who has yet to experience any of life's bitter moments, someone who knows nothing of suffering, poverty, hardship, or ill health."

But it wasn't a young, untried man who said it, rather a seasoned veteran in his sixties who had suffered beatings, imprisonments, personal conflicts, job pressures, and a thorn in the flesh. Paul the Apostle made this bold declaration: "I have strength for all things in Christ Who empowers me—I am ready for anything and equal to anything through Him Who infuses inner strength into me, [that is, I am self-sufficient in Christ's sufficiency]" (Philippians 4:13, AMP).

How could a man with both feet on the ground make a statement like that? Paul had no assurance that the future would not bring more severe trials than the past, yet he looked ahead with confidence. What revelations and experiences had developed such sinew of character and confidence of spirit in this indomitable little man?

Paul's secret: contentment

In the verses preceding Paul's confident statement we find some insight. Contentment seems to be a key. The word *contentment* is used in two ways in the New Testament. The first, an attitude of mind of being satisfied with our current situation, creates a picture of erecting a barricade around ourselves and declaring that what God has given or not given "is enough." When it comes to externals, we are content with what is inside our barricade; we need not reach outside to be complete.

"It is enough." We don't hear that thought expressed very often. The human condition is one characterized by a lack of contentment. More often we hear, "If only." The great Episcopal prayer, "Give us minds always contented with our present condition," reminds us to say, "It is enough."

The Bible teaches that contentment is an important Christian virtue. After John the Baptist preached repentance to the crowds, some soldiers asked him what they should do to demonstrate repentance. John replied, "Don't extort money and don't accuse people falsely—be content with your pay" (Luke 3:14). Be fair and be satisfied.

Later in the New Testament, Paul fine tuned a young pastor's perspective on life. He warned Timothy that some use religion as a money-making business, and added, "But godliness with contentment is great gain. For we brought nothing into the world, and we can take nothing out of it. But if we have food and clothing, we will be content with that" (1 Timothy 6:6-8). The desire for "more" tempts and traps and plunges men into "ruin and destruction," but a godly, satisfied life is of great value.

The writer of the book of Hebrews concludes his letter with a few final instructions. He tells us to be content with what we have because God has emphatically pledged to be faithful to us:

> I will not in any way fail you nor give you up nor leave you without support. [I will] not, [I will] not, [I will] not in any degree leave you helpless, nor forsake nor let [you] down, [relax My hold on you].—Assuredly not!" (Hebrews 13:5, AMP).

Paul's life is an example of godliness with contentment. He said, "I know what it is to be in need, and I know what it is to have plenty. I have learned the secret of being content in any and every situation, whether well fed or hungry, whether living in plenty or in want" (Philippians 4:12). Paul lived with a certain detachment from his circumstances, content with what God brought his way. But this explains only part of what Paul meant by contentment.

In the New Testament there is a second word translated *content* that has a different shade of meaning. It is used only once in the Bible. Paul stated, "I have learned to be content whatever the circumstances" (Philippians 4:11). *Content* here means self-sufficient. Self-sufficiency was a favorite theme of the Stoics, a sect that taught man should be complete in himself, unmoved by the circumstances of life. When Paul used the word *content,* he meant being adequate for life because of Christ's life in him. A kindred noun in 2 Corinthians 9:8 amplifies the idea of self-sufficiency: "And God is able to make all grace abound to you, so that in all things at all times, having all that you need, you will abound in every good work."

How Paul developed this attitude

But how did Paul develop the attitude of being satisfied with what God brought his way, and gain the confidence that he was self-sufficient in Christ? Paul indicated that he learned contentment. In Philippians 4:11, the word *learned* carries the idea of initiation as practiced by the sects.

My husband tells me that during his initiation into a fraternity in college, he was required to stand beneath a second-story window with his mouth open and swallow a raw egg dropped from above by an upperclassman. When his turn came,

Roger felt the strange sensation of the egg slipping down his throat. But not until later when the pledges were required to run to the next phase of the ceremony, did he realize that the egg had slipped down his shirt, not into his mouth. He had *not* been fully initiated.

The initiation Paul spoke of is not a light-hearted induction: "For it seems to me that God has put us apostles on display at the end of the procession, like men condemned to die in the arena. We have been made a spectacle to the whole universe, to angels as well as to men" (1 Corinthians 4:9). To undergo hardship for Christ's sake was Paul's initiation.

The verb tense used in verse eleven indicates that Paul learned this meaning of contentment at a point in time. This doesn't nullify the idea of process, but only communicates that at some point his understanding finally jelled. After years of experiencing God and learning from Him, an awareness penetrated Paul—"I am self-sufficient in Christ." But the light did not dawn in a vacuum. How did this truth penetrate with such force?

In the book of 2 Corinthians, penned approximately eight years before the Philippian letter, Paul revealed, as nowhere else, the extent of stress, persecution, and hardship he endured. This book gives us some idea of the kinds of experiences and lessons that may have developed Paul's confidence. Paul wrote,

> I have worked much harder, been in prison more frequently, been flogged more severely,

and been exposed to death again and again. Five times I received from the Jews the forty lashes minus one. Three times I was beaten with rods, once I was stoned, three times I was shipwrecked, I spent a night and a day in the open sea, I have been constantly on the move. I have been in danger from rivers, in danger from bandits, in danger from my own countrymen, in danger from Gentiles; in danger in the city, in danger in the country, in danger at sea; and in danger from false brothers. I have labored and toiled and have often gone without sleep; I have known hunger and thirst and have often gone without food; I have been cold and naked. Besides everything else, I face daily the pressures of my concern for all the churches. (2 Corinthians 11:23-28).

If we were to read this account in a Marvel Comic or a far-fetched adventure novel, we might wink at the author's penchant for exaggeration. But this was real life, not fiction; the Apostle Paul, not a superhero, enduring more than mere man is thought capable of enduring. Anybody's emotional stamina would have been tested, and Paul wasn't strong physically. How then, did he overcome such odds? What was this weak man's survival secret?

Paul knew he was weak, and that weakness was no disadvantage: "Therefore I will boast all the more gladly about my weaknesses, so that Christ's power may rest on me. That is why, for Christ's sake, I delight in weakness, in insults, in hardships, in persecutions, in difficulties. For when I am weak, then I am strong" (2 Corinthians 12:9-10). Paul had heard the Lord say, "My grace is sufficient for you, for my power is made perfect in weakness" (2 Corinthians 12:8). Echoing the same truth, Charles H. Spurgeon, an English preacher during the 19th century, said, "Empty buckets are fittest for the well of grace."[1]

Perhaps Paul was as awed by his survival as we are. As he nursed tender cuts, welts, and bruises after another beating, flogging, or stoning, he had ample time to reflect on his own weakness, the seriousness of the situation he had just come through, and the mighty working of God on his behalf. Paul learned experiencially that if God's grace was always available, and if his own weakness was the purest channel to carry God's strength, then he had at his disposal all he needed for whatever lay ahead.

Lessons for our life
Like Paul, we face an unknown future. We do not know what the days ordained for us contain, but we can prepare for whatever lies ahead.

View life as a learning opportunity. Ask God what He wants you to learn from the situations you face. Daily Bible reading and prayer prepare us to receive instruction and direction from God. When we set aside specific time to listen, He often encourages us with His Presence and promises, and interprets to some degree the circumstances of life. Take advantage of the natural lull after hard times when you're pulling together the pieces to sort through the events and ferret out the lessons. Sometimes the only thing that you can conclude is that God is to be trusted even though you find no answers.

The situations we face today can build a greater God confidence in our life and give us assurance that in Christ we can tackle what lies ahead. Incident after incident, lesson after lesson, year after year, as we experience God's great faithfulness, grace, and power, we will gain the confidence to say, "I can do all things through Christ who gives me strength." Paul said,

> We do not want you to be uninformed, brothers, about the hardships we suffered in the province of Asia. We were under great pressure, far beyond our ability to endure, so that we despaired even of life. Indeed, in our hearts we felt the sentence of death. But this happened that we might not rely on ourselves but on God, who raises the dead. He has delivered us from such a deadly peril, and he will deliver us (2 Corinthians 1:8-10).

Tough times. Paul was stretched beyond his human capacity, yet he experienced deliverance. From the abyss Paul asked not, "Why me, Lord?" but "What do you want me to understand from this situation?" Paul concluded that everything happened "that we might not rely on ourselves but on God."

Phillips Brooks, Rector of the Trinity Church of Boston in the 1800s wrote,

In every true sorrow of his there is something which only God "who hath made heaven and earth" can comfort; and that in every weakness of his there is something which only God "who hath made heaven and earth" can help. . . . The final purpose of all consolation and help is revelation. The reason why we are led into trouble and out again is not merely that we may value happiness the more from having lost it once and found it again, but that we may know something which we could not know except by that teaching, that we may bear upon our nature some impress which could not have been stamped except on natures just so softened to receive it.[2]

Few people lean on God when they feel they can handle circumstances themselves. Usually situations force us into dependence because we're in over our head. Paul despaired of life and relied on God for deliverance.

When troubles come, we seek escape, and sometimes accept any escape or relief. We may plunge ourselves into our work, or "run away" through excessive sleep, fascinating travel, or a change of location or company. Relief may come in many forms, but true comfort comes from God alone. Other means of relief can keep us too busy to feel the pain, or can sedate us, dulling the sensation of pain, but only God provides deep, rich comfort in the midst of suffering. He pours out grace and mercy and pulls back the curtains of revelation that we might see His character and purposes more clearly. Troubled times can bring revelation and comfort of a depth that our own solutions never provide.

Charles H. Spurgeon said, "As sure as ever God puts His children in the furnace, he will be in the furnace with them."[3] Surely Paul experienced this help when he and Silas sang praises to God from a dark, dank prison in Philippi after receiving a severe beating. We may safely rely on the God who promises to be present with us. No one else will always be there.

In itself, the process of waiting on God in hard times accomplishes something in our life. As we wait, dependent, acknowledging our personal destitution and absolute need, our state of soul makes us spiritually receptive and alert. Time spent considering the divine purposes of our trials brings more complete understanding of who God is. Paul learned that as he relied on God in every trial, he was strengthened and sustained. He not only endured, but he received some spiritual blessing or insight for himself, and to pass on to others.

Pressures and persecutions assaulted Paul. Yet, in him we do not find a man biting the bullet or pulling himself up by his bootstraps. Paul was sustained and empowered by Another's life in him:

> But we have this treasure in jars of clay to show that this all-surpassing power is from God and not from us. We are hard pressed on every side, but not crushed; perplexed, but not in despair; persecuted, but not abandoned; struck down, but not destroyed. We always carry around in

our body the death of Jesus, so that the life of Jesus may also be revealed in our body. For we who are alive are always being given over to death for Jesus' sake, so that his life may be revealed in our mortal body (2 Corinthians 4:7-11).

Ken, a friend of ours, and his wife and toddler son were in an auto accident in Europe. Ken's wife was killed and his son, Luke, sustained injuries that left his lower body paralyzed. Returning to the States, Ken resumed his job, and faced grief and loneliness along with the numerous demands of caring for Luke: therapy sessions, endless rounds of doctor's appointments, caring for their everyday needs, exercising Luke's lifeless limbs. Reading letters of Ken's typical day wore me out. I said to my husband, "How can he go on? I'm so worried for him. Surely he can't keep this up much longer."

Then my husband reminded me, "In Exodus, the amazing thing wasn't that the bush was on fire, but that it wasn't consumed." The amazing thing with Ken, also, was that he wasn't consumed. The life of Christ within him sustained and heartened Ken.

God's all-surpassing power keeps us from being crushed or destroyed. This power delivers us from troubles without and from corruption within:

His divine power has given us everything we need for life and godliness through our knowledge of him who called us by his own glory and goodness. Through these he has given us his very great and precious promises, so that through them you may participate in the divine nature and escape the corruption in the world caused by evil desires (2 Peter 1:3-4).

The struggles you face may not be shipwreck, but boredom; not beatings, but schedule pressures; not imprisonment, but the illusion that you can manage life without Christ. These trials have the potential to destroy or establish your faith.

A few years ago, we had a series of break-ins to our home. The losses were small, but irritating; replacing broken windows was time consuming; and the emotional upheavals were draining. We felt helpless and violated. But God helped us gain an enriching perspective on the problem.

When we focused our attention on the Lord, we no longer felt like victims, but rather we felt like people safe within a sovereign God's control. We realized *God is all-knowing.* He knew who did it, why they did it, and how the burglars could be caught and helped. He knew what he wanted us to learn from the experience, and how it could bring Him glory. God knew the feelings (upsets) we experienced. He knew how much we could take.

We realized *God is all-powerful.* He could stop the burglaries. He could sustain us even if they lasted until we died. He could use this for good in our lives and to promote the gospel (Philippians 1:12). He could protect us and our things, or He could take them all.

We realized *God is love*. He loves us and nothing will touch our lives except if His love permits it. The break-ins were part of our lives because He loves us. And He loves the burglars. Like Paul through his initiation, we learned:

Weakness is no detriment.

God's grace is sufficient.

The power to endure is from God.

We must rely on Him.

These lessons are warp and woof of a new fabric, a deeper resolve. To paraphrase Paul, "It has dawned on me that I have in myself in Christ everything I need for all circumstances."

Notes

1. Charles H. Spurgeon, *The Treasury of Spurgeon* (Grand Rapids, Michigan: Baker Book House, 1967), page 38.

2. Phillips Brooks, *The Candle of the Lord* (London: MacMillan Publishing Company, 1884), pages 271-272.

3. Spurgeon, page 45.

9
A Pilgrim Mentality

Most men choose Heaven above hell, but Abraham chose Heaven above earth. This choice gave perspective to the trials of life and made his life surprisingly and singularly free of distraction as he steadfastly focused his gaze on God. He had much of what the world seeks, yet none of this diverted him from total commitment to God. The abundance Abraham received from God's hand never became a sidetrack from the journey towards Heaven.

Life was not easy for him; he had tests as severe as any man. But shining through was a quality of life seen only in those who have come to a realization of a deeper reality. The secret of his spiritual stature: a pilgrim perspective born out of faith.

I read *Pilgrim's Progress* once. Now after twenty-some years as a Christian, I'm wondering about my progress as a pilgrim. I don't hear the word *pilgrim* used very much. Has God called twentieth-century Christians to be pilgrims? If so, what characterizes the pilgrim?

An early pilgrim said, "By the grace of God I am a Christian man, by my actions a great sinner, and by calling a homeless wanderer of the humblest birth who roams from place to place. My worldly goods are a knapsack with some dried bread in it on my back, and in my breastpocket a Bible. And that is all."[1]

Must the Christian be able to cram all his earthly possessions into a backpack? Or can a pilgrim have a new carpet in his house or a camper in the driveway? Are prosperity and pilgrimage incompatible?

Residence here; citizenship above

The word *pilgrim* in the Greek means *resident foreigner;* that description fits Abraham well. Although God gave Abraham and his posterity the most important piece of land in the world—God Himself setting the geographic boundaries—Abraham never clutched that land to his breast as his possession, "for he was looking forward to the city with foundations, whose architect and builder is God" (Hebrews 11:10). Important territory (we recognize it as strategic, even today), but Abraham set his eyes on a much better land. He camped here, but was always conscious that his home was Heaven.

Faith
Faith is the essential ingredient in pilgrim living—"being sure of what we hope for and certain of what we do not see. This is what the ancients were commended for" (Hebrews 11:1).

God told Abraham to follow Him and He would do great things through and for him. God gave Abraham superlative promises, but neglected to fill in any of the details. The scope of the promises was awesome, yet Abraham believed God and moved on the basis of His promises and commands. Neither the immensity of the problem, nor the apparent impossibility of the promise, deterred Abraham from faith. Though he was "as good as dead," he believed he would become the father of multitudes, as God promised.

Abraham lived here on earth as a pilgrim because he was fully persuaded that God would care for his needs. He left the sophisticated city of Ur to follow the Lord, knowing He would provide. With this confidence he gave his nephew Lot first choice of the land. With this confidence he prepared to sacrifice his son as a burnt offering. As father and son climbed the mountain, Isaac asked his father, "Where is the lamb?" God provided a lamb at the last moment, so Abraham called that place in the region of Moriah "The Lord will provide."

Route conscious, not root conscious
"By faith he [Abraham] made his home in the promised land like a stranger in a foreign country" (Hebrews 11:9). This is incredible. The phrases

made his home, in the promised land, and *like a stranger in a foreign country* are startling. By faith he made his home there, yet remained a pilgrim. He fluffed the comforter on his bed, mended his leaky roof, ordered the books on his shelf, cut a bud for the vase on his table, yet focused all the while on his eternal home. The realization that his home on earth was temporary didn't demand austerity, but it did assign value.

Thoreau lamented, "We now no longer camp as for a night, but have settled down on earth and forgotten heaven."[2] But not so Abraham. He was geographically and spiritually where God wanted him. He made his home in the Promised Land, but sent down no roots there. Mobility and availability characterized His life. (Sometime count the number of times poor Sarah pulled up tent pegs and followed her pilgrim husband.) God also called Isaac and Jacob to rootless existences.

The prosperous pilgrim

Abraham was a pilgrim, but he couldn't get all his possessions in his backpack. When he left Haran, he and his family took "all the possessions they had accumulated and the people they had acquired" with them (Genesis 12:5). Later, when they left Egypt, they took everything again: Abraham "had become very wealthy in livestock and in silver and gold" (Genesis 13:2).

But Abraham didn't seek riches, or make decisions based on personal gain. Even after he risked his life storming into the enemy camp to free Lot and the captives from Sodom, he refused to accept any payment from the King of Sodom. He would make no alliance with that kind of man. The King of Sodom would never say, "I made Abraham rich" (see Genesis 14). Materialism did not blur his principles or blunt his conscience.

When he allowed his nephew Lot first choice of the land, Abraham demonstrated an open-handed disposition that characterized his life. He fixed his eyes on eternal realities instead of searching for the best deal here. Only at God's command, "Lift up your eyes," did Abraham focus briefly on the territory.

Abraham had great wealth, but unlike the rich young ruler who would not sell his possessions (see Mark 10:17-22), he would have given it up without question. How do I know that? Abraham did not withhold his dear son of promise, Isaac. The truth of Romans 8:32 holds true in this case as well: "He . . . did not spare his own Son, but gave him up."

Never look back

When Abraham departed from Ur to follow God to an unknown land, he left a thriving city. Excavations reveal Ur to have been a city of refinement and comfort. Delicately finished vessels of gold have been found in graves as old as 4000 B.C. However, if Abraham did think of the country he left, God says he would have had opportunity to return to it:

> All these people [including Abraham] were still living by faith when they died. They did not

receive the things promised; they only saw them and welcomed them from a distance. And they admitted that they were aliens and strangers on earth. People who say such things show that they are looking for a country of their own. If they had been thinking of the country they had left, they would have had opportunity to return. Instead, they were longing for a better country—a heavenly one. Therefore God is not ashamed to be called their God, for he has prepared a city for them (Hebrews 11:13-16).

These true pilgrims never looked back with wistful gazes, but focused on the eternal and superior country God had promised them.

No matter. I've got better coming

The book of Hebrews pays tribute to those, like Abraham, who knew they had better coming. They endured with joy, because they had glimpsed something more real awaiting them. Of them, the writer of Hebrews says they joyfully accepted the confiscation of their property, because they knew they had better and lasting possessions (see Hebrews 10:34).

Like them, Marcella, a woman of Roman nobility (325-410), used her wealth to further the Kingdom of Christ on earth. In 410 AD, the Goths attacked Rome and surged into her garden to plunder her. Marcella died shortly after from the beating she received at their hands, rejoicing that her treasure was laid up in Heaven out of reach of marauders. I can imagine her saying, "They didn't get a thing. I sent it all ahead."

Moses knew that he had better than what Egypt could offer. He chose to be mistreated with the children of God rather than to enjoy the pleasures and privileges of Egypt: "He regarded disgrace for the sake of Christ as of greater value than the treasures of Egypt, because he was looking ahead to his reward" (Hebrews 11:26).

Jesus, too, looked ahead: "Who for the joy set before him endured the cross, scorning its shame" (Hebrews 12:2). And so did Paul: "I consider that our present sufferings are not worth comparing with the glory that will be revealed in us" (Romans 8:18). Others "were tortured and refused to be released, so that they might gain a better resurrection" (Hebrews 11:35). For these faithful ones, nothing here was good enough to capture their affections or to divert them from a better country.

But what about me?

A well-known hymn includes the words *pilgrim through this barren land*. But often the land is opulent, flourishing, tempting. It is undoubtedly easier to keep the pilgrim mentality in the desert than in the oasis, and far easier to set the heart and mind on Heaven when living in a parched and meager land. Richard Halverson, chaplain of the United States Senate, made a disturbing comparison: "The apostolic church dreamed of the Kingdom of their Lord and Savior Jesus Christ. They believed in it, laid down their lives for that Kingdom. There was nothing in this world good enough for them. That's not true today. We never had it so good."[3]

The pilgrim faces an inner tension precisely because he is called to be *in* a world contrary to the Kingdom, but not *of* that world. He is left in the world as a representative of another Kingdom, serving another Master, endeavoring to present His claim to a world in rebellion. The tension is total because these two kingdoms can never be reconciled. Man cannot serve two masters.

History is strewn with promising, potential pilgrims who were unable to sever ties with the kingdom of this world. The imprisoned Paul was deserted by Demas "because he loved this world" (2 Timothy 4:10). Lot begged to be allowed to enter the town of Zoar after the destruction of Sodom because he was unwilling to endure hardship. Solomon, in spite of his great wisdom, ran his fingers through his glittering treasures and the tresses of his many wives, and lost sight of the Kingdom. The rich young ruler went away sad because his wealth dulled his view of the eternal.

Because we, too, are imperfect, floundering pilgrims at best, living in a hostile environment in which the Kingdom has not yet been fully revealed, we must acknowledge the tensions that exist and come to terms with the fact that we are in process. Enemies of the pilgrim life surround us; we must commit ourselves to the process of pilgrimage.

Developing a pilgrim mentality

To develop a pilgrim mentality, we must first gaze on our pilgrim Savior. Jesus left the glories of Heaven, the perfect home, to become flesh and live among us. He was born in an unsanitary stable, lived in the home of parents of humble circumstances, in a town of questionable reputation. He had no home of His own, no wealth, no position in society. When confronted with the possibility of becoming an earthly king, He escaped man's intention and fled to the hills. He knew Himself to be a heavenly king, yet resided as a pilgrim on earth. The Gospels make it very clear: Jesus lived on earth for thirty-three years, but His home was Heaven. And although He lived on this planet as man, His life bore the stamp of another realm.

The stamp of another realm

If we are to bear the same stamp, we must be transformed. In Romans 12:2 we read, "Do not conform any longer to the pattern of this world, but be transformed by the renewing of your mind." We don't have to do anything to be conformed to this world, but to be transformed requires a work of God.

God faithfully works by His Spirit and His Word to chip away what is untrue and unworthy and to remold our mind. To develop a pilgrim mentality, we must allow God's Word to reprogram our thinking, and His abundant promises to enlarge our vision. Every sojourner needs close, regular contact with the Bible to remain a stranger here. This world tramples the tender bud of pilgrim desire, but God's Word strengthens our pilgrim resolve by nourishing our feeblest endeavors and giving us a foretaste of glory that fortifies us for the pilgrimage.

In Deuteronomy 17:18-20, God commanded that the king write himself a copy of God's law and keep it with him to read all the days of his life, so that he would revere and obey the Lord and live humbly among his brothers. A man in power can easily begin to believe that he is wiser and more worthy than his fellows. Only the jolt of a daily dose of spiritual reality can keep him in touch with the truth that he is merely a man, a shadow, a mist, a flower withering in the sun. God's Word provides the gentle pressure or the high-voltage shock needed to keep the Kingdom before him and help him view this present world with perspective.

A pilgrim quickly becomes earthbound unless the Bible, the double-edged Sword, slices through his bindings. Apart from the freeing influence of the Word, the pilgrim becomes—like Gulliver—tied to earth without his knowledge. The pilgrim's perceptions become distorted, his values twisted, and his goals unworthy of his heavenly calling.

In Psalm 84 the songwriter expressed the heart of the spiritual sojourner. His soul "yearns, even faints" to be near God. His heart and flesh "cry out for the living God." This pilgrim even envies the sparrows who nest in the temple, because he knows that greatest joy is experienced in God's presence.

Verse five says that those "who have set their hearts on pilgrimage" are the happy ones. That phrase speaks of the pilgrim process. The pilgrim has such a deep yearning for God that he thinks continually about his next trip to the temple, and in his mind as he works, walks, or sits by his wife at night, he is there. His heart and mind are on the eternal. He exemplifies the charge given in Colossians to "set your hearts on things above" (3:1) and to "set your minds on things above, not on earthly things" (3:2).

This man's longing to be in the Lord's presence flavors all of life. The events of his life are seen through eyes that focus elsewhere. There is more to life than just what each day brings. He is motivated and strengthened by unseen realities, by something outside his immediate circumstance. This pilgrim has a perspective that the earthbound miss. And when he passes through the desert, he makes it a place of springs (see Psalm 84:6). Even in the dry places he finds pools.

The psalmist declared that pilgrims "go from strength to strength till each appears before God in Zion" (Psalm 54:7). Those who set their hearts on pilgrimage are infused with strength, and nourished and enriched by God. Their eternal focus gives perspective for today's trials and a reason for continuing when times are tough. No wonder the psalmist wrote, "Better is one day in your courts than a thousand elsewhere; I would rather be a doorkeeper in the house of my God than dwell in the tents of the wicked" (Psalm 84:10).

How does the pilgrim learn to focus on the eternal? Our spiritual disciplines can be so weighted down by the force of gravity that our gaze barely makes it to the horizon. Bible study can become academic homework, our devotions more like an exercise of form than spiritual experience, our prayers just dry duty. J. H. Jowett prayed, "Transform our spiritual habits that we may find ourselves able to fix our minds upon the things above."[4] But what kind of transformation of our spiritual habits will enable us to fix our attention above?

Instead of thinking of Bible study as our findings gleaned and jotted down on the paper before us, we might profitably reflect on the fact that the Holy Spirit is our teacher, our private tutor, present to uncover mystery and unfold truth to us. And our Risen Lord is seated at the Father's right hand, interceding for us, praying that our heart will be enlarged to receive His words, that we might become like Him.

In our quiet times, we can focus on God waiting expectantly for that time of fellowship. The Bible says our prayers are like incense rising up to God. Imagine Him inhaling their fragrance with delight. Remember that real prayer originates with Him as He moves us to pray and then stirs within us expressions from His own heart.

The same reflection could enhance our attendance at worship services, times of fellowship with other believers, and attempts to communicate the Lord to those who don't know Him.

A pilgrim has one citizenship

When pioneer missionary Hudson Taylor immersed himself in China's culture in the 1800s (he even shaved his head and grew a long pigtail), Christian missions gave renewed consideration to adapting the missionary to the culture he hoped to reach. Important as this is, the critical issue is that he learns what it means to be a Christian in that culture. A Christian should be distinctive in any culture. Our goal in missions must not be to make missionaries more Mexican or Indonesian or Siberian, but more thoroughly Christian. The Christian is a pilgrim at home or in a foreign land. His citizenship is in Heaven, and the culture of that Kingdom must immerge as predominant.

Our lives do not express clear, pure Christianity. To varying degrees, our thinking and values have been influenced by our immediate culture. No matter how desperately we want to live according to His Kingdom, we find that we see through a glass darkly. Our citizenship is in a Kingdom radically divergent from the world we inhabit. Our King tells us, "Blessed are the poor in spirit . . . blessed are those who mourn . . . whoever wants to become great must become a servant . . . whoever wants to save his life will lose it, but whoever loses his life for me will find it." But the words of our King are not easily grasped or absorbed into practice in any culture.

Be rich toward God

A pilgrim recognizes his wealth in Christ and seeks to be rich toward God. Jesus warned against all kinds of greed by telling the parable of the rich fool. This man thought life consisted in the abundance of his possessions, but he never reached the saturation point. How curious that the rich would always be happy to have more. The rich fool concentrated on accumulating wealth, and gave inadequate attention to his soul. He died and reaped the devastation. Jesus said, "This is how it will be with anyone who stores up things for himself but is not rich toward God" (Luke 12:21).

The Scriptures warn again and again against trusting in wealth. Psalm 49 paints a vivid picture of the futility of trusting in riches. Wealth cannot ransom a man's soul. Wise and foolish alike leave their wealth behind when they die. Even those "significant" enough to have institutions or places named after them, or to have built princely mansions still end up decaying in graves.

Jesus said, "I tell you the truth, it is hard for a rich man to enter the kingdom of heaven" (Matthew 19:23). So Paul instructed,

> Command those who are rich in this present world not to be arrogant or to put their hope in wealth, which is so uncertain, but to put their hope in God, who richly provides us with everything for our enjoyment (1 Timothy 6:17-19).

Jesus' life perfectly illustrates the pilgrim perspective:

> Unique in Christ is not his renunciation of earth's costliness or the taking upon himself of all sorts of privations, but that he is free as no one has ever been before or since. Christ's greatness lies in his perfect freedom, that is clear and sufficient unto itself. Wonderfully free as he is of all desire, of all worry about property or livelihood, he is equally untouched by all cramp

of opposition to things, of renunciation, and above all, of even the most unconscious resentment towards things he himself does not enjoy. This freedom is so natural to him that it almost escapes the attention; only gradually do we learn to recognize and appreciate it. Jesus' eye rests calmly on all things; he does not ignore beauty, but frankly accepts it for what it is: beautiful; and the good things of life for what they are: good. But all his powers of appreciation and love are directed to God with a naturalness that is the pure fruit of his union with God (as is all Christian "naturalness": not the beginning of effort, but its fulfillment).[5]

Jesus richly enjoyed all of life without trusting in or becoming enamored with things. He was free from distraction. An over-concern on the side of either austerity or prosperity can distract. Preoccupation with acquiring material goods perpetuates a destructive whirlwind; attempting to repudiate the material world propels man to seek Walden. The pilgrim perspective lies somewhere between Walden and the whirlwind. Paul spoke of this freedom when he wrote,

What I mean, brothers, is that the time is short. From now on those who have wives should live as if they had none; those who mourn, as if they did not; those who are happy, as if they were not; those who buy something, as if it were not theirs to keep; those who use the things of the world, as if not engrossed in them. For this

world in its present form is passing away
(1 Corinthians 7:29-31).

Our material world can rob or enrich, detract from or enhance our life and ministry. To richly enjoy without becoming engrossed or trusting in this present world is part of the pilgrim task.

In the parable of the rich fool, Jesus spoke of being "rich toward God." What does that mean?

Trust not in riches, but in God.
Like Abraham, believe God.
Trust Him to provide.
Embrace His promises.
Obey His directives.
Put your roots down into God and draw
security from Him.
Make decisions based on eternal realities, not
personal gain.
Store up treasure in Heaven that cannot be
touched by thieves or corrupted by decay.
Focus your attention above.
Dwell on the eternal blessings you possess.

Therefore, since we are receiving a kingdom that cannot be shaken, let us be thankful, and so worship God acceptably with reverence and awe, for our God is a consuming fire (Hebrews 12:28). For here we do not have an enduring city, but we are looking for the city that is to come (Hebrews 13:14).

Notes
1. R.M. French, trans., *The Way of the Pilgrim*

(Minneapolis, Minnesota: The Seabury Press, 1952), page 1.

2. Henry David Thoreau, *Walden and Other Writings* (New York: Bantam Books, 1962), pages 132-133.

3. Richard C. Halverson, "Why Should God Visit Us . . . When We're Not Interested?" *Christianity Today,* November 12, 1982, page 52.

4. J.H. Jowett, *The Whole Armour of God* (London: Hodder and Stoughton, 1916), page 98.

5. Romano Guardini, *The Lord* (Chicago: Henry Regnery Company, 1954), pages 280-281.